Simply ORGANISED

An expert's guide to decluttering your life and home

AMY REVELL

First published by Busybird Publishing 2016

Copyright © 2019 Amy Revell

ISBN
Print: 978-1-925949-57-5

Amy Revell has asserted her right under the Copyright, Designs and Patents Act 1988 to be identified as the author of this work. The information in this book is based on the author's experiences and opinions. The publisher specifically disclaims responsibility for any adverse consequences, which may result from use of the information contained herein. Permission to use information has been sought by the author. Any breaches will be rectified in further editions of the book.

All rights reserved. No part of this publication may be reproduced, stored in or introduced into a retrieval system, or transmitted in any form, or by any means (electronic, mechanical, photocopying, recording or otherwise) without the prior written permission of the author. Any person who does any unauthorised act in relation to this publication may be liable to criminal prosecution and civil claims for damages. Enquiries should be made through the publisher.

Cover image: Jessica Lee
Cover design: Amy Revell
Prime Motivator: Jesse Revell
Chief Encourager: Elijah Revell
Best Business Partner: Kirsty Farrugia
Layout and typesetting: Busybird Publishing
Editor: Beau Hillier

Busybird Publishing
2/118 Para Road
Montmorency, Victoria
Australia 3094
www.busybird.com.au

To my best friend and husband Cal. Never would I have dreamed of marrying a man so gracious and trusting that you would give wings to all my dreams. You believe in me, release me, support me and sometimes laugh at my silly ideas. Thank you for loving me for who I am and not what I achieve.

Journeying through life with you is crazy fun. You're a brilliant dad to Jesse and Elijah, you're an important part of our extended family and you're a loving pastor to our church. You're the best and I can't wait to see what new adventure our future holds.

Client Testimonials

'Clearing out my art room was a job I'd been avoiding as I simply didn't know where to start. Amy went above and beyond, researching possible storage solutions before the momentous culling and organising even began, and her enthusiasm motivated me to continue the decluttering in many other areas of my work and home! I couldn't recommend her services highly enough!'

– **Sally Cotterill**

'I am feeling so excited today after having Amy reorganise my pantry in my new kitchen. I was feeling so overwhelmed and couldn't seem to fit everything in to my new pantry. Wow! What a transformation! Not only do I have more space but I will save money! I can see everything clearly and hopefully now I can stop doubling up at the supermarket.'

– **Jessica Winnell**

'We recently moved into our new home. I was getting overwhelmed by the task of finding the right home for all our stuff, which had been hastily moved from our rental and never really put away properly. Amy provided great guidance and pleasant company while we sorted through the stuff over a few sessions. This helped me get inspired and motivated to continue the process on my own, too.

'Perhaps more significantly, I then hired Amy to help my seven year old daughter get her room sorted out. Miss Seven has always been a bit of a hoarder and we'd had a lot of conflict about getting rid of bits and pieces and keeping her room tidy. Amy worked with her over two sessions and completely transformed her room! It's been over a week now and I have actually "caught" my daughter tidying her room after bedtime. She now "gets it" – the joy of having a clear and peaceful space!

'Now of course Miss Nine is asking for Amy's help, too!'
    – Brooke Noble

'I'm not a naturally organised person and was living in "chaos". Hubby and I were ready to install new kitchen cupboards due to lack of space. Once Amy came through and helped me reorganise my kitchen we no longer need more cupboards, as everything fit coherently! I love working in my new organised space and everything just seems to make sense. Would happily have Amy over again to help with other rooms. Money well spent!'
    – Miriam Robertson

Contents

Introduction	i
1. Devices	1
2. Toys	9
3. Kitchen	21
4. Wardrobe	33
BONUS SECTION ONE: Organised Car	42
5. Housework	45
6. Gifts	57
7. Paperwork	67
BONUS SECTION TWO: Kids Artwork	80
8. Garage and Junk Room	83
9. Sentimental Items	93
BONUS SECTION THREE: Organised Medications	102
10. Storage	105
BONUS SECTION FOUR: Organised Laundry	116
11. Getting Organised	119
12. Minimalism	129
Afterword	137
About the Author	139
The Art of Decluttering	141
Podcast	142
Services	143
Events	144

Introduction

My organising story started about thirty years ago, when I was entering primary school. School was perfect for me – it was organised, structured and we were encouraged to be neat in the work we produced.

I quickly learnt that my bent in school was toward efficiency rather than perfection. If I could finish a project with time left at the end and still receive a high mark, I was thrilled. Even though I was an A grade student, I was more interested in fitting more into my busy schedule than working that bit harder to become an A+ student.

This became particularly evident in senior school where, during my last two years of high school, I also enjoyed a busy extracurricular schedule. I was the music captain, the sports house captain, was on the debating team, was part of Amnesty International, was part of our local youth group, played in the school jazz band, took private piano lessons, sung in the school choir, performed in the school musical, worked a part time job and had a social life to boot. At our Year 12 valedictory dinner I was presented with the award for the busiest student in the year level.

Multitasking and finding efficient ways to do simple tasks became second nature. Organising and decluttering followed naturally as I got married, moved out of home and started my own family. I've always enjoyed feeling organised, but as life got busier I discovered that it was also saving me time, money and headspace.

I took a job as an office manager at twenty-one and realised that my organisational skills weren't something that everyone had. I loved helping other people be more efficient and productive. I had several roles as an executive assistant and the satisfaction in helping organise someone else's time and schedule was incredibly rewarding.

When I became a mother I continued to work part time and my need for an organised home increased exponentially. I didn't want going back to work to become stressful, so I just made sure everything was organised (as well as possible with a newborn baby!). This enjoyment for organisation flowed into keeping toys and everything needed to look after a busy family in order. As our family grew, so did my passion for the benefits of a simple, organised life.

I love moving house – I love the decluttering and packing and I love setting up home at the other end. Moving house with a four month old taught me some great decluttering skills, because I didn't want to pack anything we didn't absolutely have to take with us. Fast forward to today and I enjoy working with beautiful women around the country, doing something I'm so passionate about. I get the privilege of helping women to organise and declutter their homes.

And this is where you come in. I wanted to share the love far and wide – to inspire and encourage women of all walks of life to take back control of their homes and lives. We're all busy women; whether you're a business owner, single working mum or stay at

: *Introduction*

home mum, the demands on our time are varied, but one thing unifies us ... we all want to live a more organised life.

Rather than forge this journey alone, allow me to lead you along my well beaten track to organisation. I'll hold your hand, we'll have some laughs and at the end you'll be glad you took the first step.

Devices

'How many old iPhones do you really need to keep "just in case"?'

You may not think of your electronics and devices as an area of your home that needs decluttering and organising. But more and more of these critters enter our home each year and few seem to ever escape. Electronics seem to breed in our homes – have a look around you right now. Is there a tablet? Laptop? Kindle? Mobile phone or two? Our lives are heavily reliant on electronics so we're not going to go crazy and get rid of it all, but we are going to enjoy what we have by decluttering what we don't need.

We have become a society of upgrades rather than replacements. If you've seen the animated movie *Robots* with Ewan McGregor, you'll remember the 'baddies' tricked everyone into wanting upgrades instead of fixing what was broken, because they could make more money this way. Sounds kind of familiar doesn't it? This means that instead of buying something new only when an old one breaks, we upgrade to the newest and greatest, even though our 'old' one is still in perfect working condition.

This is a pattern of consumerism that was completely unknown to our grandparents and seems to have snuck up on us while we weren't watching. This leaves a trail of working devices and electronics in our homes that can be put to better use.

Every device that enters the home comes with a charger. But keeping track of what's what can be a lot of work, so we tend to have a drawer somewhere that is a tangled mess of cords that we assume we might need one day, but hope we never do. Getting this organised will save you time and make you money in the long term (more on that later).

> *We have become a society of upgrades rather than replacements.*

According to Mobile Muster, there are an estimated 25.5 million unwanted mobile phones in homes around Australia. Environmentally you can't just chuck an old mobile in the rubbish bin; it needs to be recycled correctly. But even better than recycling it, why not sell it and make yourself some pocket money? Old mobiles are sitting in bedside tables and office drawers in already cluttered homes. How many old phones do you really need to keep 'just in case'? Phones, devices and gaming consoles can all be sold on sites like eBay, so instead of having idle items sitting around, list them online and make some pocket money for yourself.

Some devices don't leave our sides even when we take bathroom breaks; others have a permanent home (like a PC or PlayStation) and others still are packed away for use when we need them. Have a think where else electronics may be hiding in your house … in your bedside table or in the TV cabinet? Your husband's man cave is sure to have a few and even the kitchen might have a couple.

So the first thing I want you to do is to gather all your electronics from around the home and put them all on a clear kitchen table. Every single piece of electronic equipment is to be gathered together – not just your own, but everything the family owns too (with their permission). Don't disconnect things like a PC, printer or TV, but for everything that is portable, get it on the table. Gather the devices, but also gather all chargers, connective cords, charging stations, headphones – all accessories you can find.

So in front of you will now be a surprisingly large collection of portable electronics and accessories:

- Smart watches
- Phones
- Tablets
- eReaders
- Laptops
- Digital cameras
- Video cameras
- Gaming console/s
- Fitness trackers
- Other techie stuff I don't even know about!

Grab a pack of snap lock bags (I recommend the ones from Ikea as they come in many different sizes, are clear, easy to write on, have a double seal and are great value for money). In each bag place all the pieces that belong to each item. So in snap lock bag one, you might have an old mobile phone. You place in the bag the old mobile itself, as well as anything that came with it or was purchased for it. This could include a charger, headset, spare battery, phone case, etc. Then on the bag use a permanent marker to write what is inside, say 'Samsung Galaxy Model X'.

For each item, gather the accessories and put them together in a labelled bag. This may take a little while as you match cords and devices but it will make life easier. For items that you're currently using, the item itself doesn't need to live in the snap lock bag – but keeping the accessories together in one bag is going to make finding things (and eventually disposing of things) much easier.

When you're ready to replace an item, everything is together, making it easier to recycle or sell. For items that you use regularly, it's still important to have a home for them. Otherwise they'll just be left where you last used it and never fully put away.

My kids both have devices for school. These devices could just live in their school bags easily enough, but they don't. I've taught my boys to empty their school bags each night when they get home. So their lunchbox, jumper, notices, school work and the devices all come out each afternoon. The lunchbox goes in the sink, the jumper gets hung up or put in the wash, notices go on my desk where all incoming paperwork goes, and the devices are put on charge, ready for the next day.

I believe that having a home for devices is important so you know where to pack it away and also know where to find it. Many people opt to set up a charging station, which is a handy solution if you have the space.

1 . Devices

Before we even open the box of a new electronic device we grab a large snap lock bag, label it and then as we unpack the box, we place everything inside the bag. For instance, when we purchased a set of wireless headphones for the family, the snap lock bag was labelled before we even opened the box. Inside we put the warranty, and a cord we didn't need straight away. I then set up the base station at my desk where the headphones can sit and charge. If we want to connect it to the TV, I just grab the bag with that cord in it and swap it over. It's so simple, you'll be so glad you took up this habit.

I'd also recommend that you keep all these snap lock bags of devices and accessories in one place in the home, so you always know where to go when you need something. A designated drawer or large container in the cupboard is perfect.

So back to your kitchen table … once you've grouped and bagged everything, you've probably got a few random cords still sitting on the table and you have no idea what they're for. These can go straight in the rubbish. Yep, straight in the rubbish. I can almost hear the outcry ('What if I need that exact cord in six months' time?'). Chances are that if you haven't used it in the last twelve months and have no idea what it's for, it's probably safe to let it go. If by some act of Murphy's Law you do eventually need the unclaimed cord, for probably under $10 you could order it online and have it delivered to your home.

Devices that are now packed up but are no longer used, wanted or needed are now little bundles of cash sitting on your kitchen table. List them online and enjoy having less clutter and a bit more money! And the good news is that selling a device with all its accessories will fetch a higher price than if you sold the device on its own.

Electronics and devices come into our homes regularly. As such, I encourage you to get into the habit of annually going through this process of decluttering and categorising your devices and electronics, so you can more fully engage with what you have while saving money in the process.

Lastly, I just want to touch on the storage and organisation of batteries. I've found that having all batteries kept in the same place makes Christmas, birthdays and your wireless mouse dying in the middle of an important email just that bit easier to manage. If you've spent any time on Pinterest, you'll probably have seen the fishing tackle box concept. The idea is that you use a sectional container (like what you'd use for fishing) and keep each size battery in its own compartment, so you can quickly get what you need when you need it.

What most people don't realise is that batteries, like medications, need to be stored out of the reach of small children. Button batteries especially, because they fit so easily in a small mouth and can cause serious injury (and even death) if ingested.

So, make a habit of keeping all your batteries together in one container (sectional if you have one) and keep it elevated to where little hands can't reach it. For us, the container (with a lid) sits on a shelf in the laundry so it's easy to access when we need fresh batteries.

I can also see at a glance when we're running low on certain batteries and can pick some up at the shops before we actually run out and have to borrow them from another device.

Simple Tips

- Gather all electronic items and accessories on the kitchen table and put sets in labelled snap lock bags.
- Anything you no longer use, want or need can be sold online.
- Designate a spot in the house that electronics and accessories are kept – pop all the labelled snap lock bags in together.

Toys

'You don't even play with that anymore!'

Decluttering your home has physical, social and emotional benefits and there's a reason I suggest starting with toys if you have kids. Toys and games so easily build up in our homes and become a source of clutter and stress. Your kids may not feel the stress; in fact, they may be happy having their bedroom floor covered with toys. But you will find it stressful and the source of conflict.

New toys come into every family home on a regular basis. When I was growing up, the two main influxes were Christmas and birthdays, but more and more the incoming stream of 'new' seems to be steady. So unless you're intentional about how you handle the flow of these things, you'll quickly fill your home to capacity.

Living in a home where toys and games aren't organised leads to a waste of your money via broken and lost pieces. Your family's time will also be swallowed up in the constant search for game pieces and toys which have hidden themselves around your home. You'll feel like your home is constantly in a mess and lacking usable space.

Children struggle to be present when engaging with toys if there are other things vying for their attention. Being able to interact and play with another child is an important developmental milestone.

You'll notice that young toddlers tend to play alongside rather than with their friends, not able to share. But as they grow older they start to learn how to play together. Mindful play is often replaced with multitasking play, which isn't ideal for growing little brains. Learning to share, negotiate and play together with friends is hugely important in our children's development.

You'll no doubt notice that when children have fewer toys to play with, they seem to play better. Divided attention and having too many options can be overwhelming for children (playback: 'Mum, I'm bored. I have nothing to play with,' even though they have more toys than anyone you know).

I'm always amazed at how when we spend an afternoon at the park the kids can be occupied for hours, building a cubby with big branches and leaves. Then they come home to their toys and claim they have nothing to play with. Sometimes the simple things in life really are the best.

Teaching children respect for possessions is important, because what starts with respect for a teddy, becomes respect for a sibling, becomes respect for a school friend – and a respectful adult knows how to treat others well and be responsible with money and possessions.

There's a lot of buzz at the moment around 'being present' and what that looks like in a fast-paced, technology-driven society. A good place to start is to help our children be present when they're playing. Instead of having the TV on in the background while three different toys are mid-use, why not turn screens off while play is happening? Instead of tipping the whole toy box on the ground, pick one toy/set for your child to play with. Being present is about focus, and it's hard to focus when there's clutter.

For primary aged children, encouraging them to finish a drawing they start or finish a board game they initiate teaches them about not only being present, but about how good it feels to finish something they begin.

Teaching children that packing up is part of the process of using a toy or game will serve them well in life. If they get all the pencils out, draw a great picture but then leave the mess on the kitchen table, they haven't finished their activity. It's not until the paper and pencils are back where they belong that the activity is finished and can be fully celebrated.

I see adults regularly who struggle with this way of thinking; they'll share a meal with their family but leave the dishes on the table and move on. Or they'll mow the lawn and leave the lawnmower in the yard rather than putting it away in the shed. It's the simple things, but fully completing an activity is an excellent discipline to learn in life.

> *Being present is about focus, and it's hard to focus when there's clutter.*

Whether you store some toys away and rotate them or do a big declutter, as my husband says, 'Less is best.' Friends of mine have a *huge* garage and have a set of shelves where toys are rotated every few months. They have them stored in plastic containers so as when one lot comes in, another lot goes back out. It's a great way of keeping the toy clutter inside to a minimum because only a select few are being played with at a time. Kids also love playing with toys they haven't seen for a while, so when a new box comes out they can't wait to open it, remember the toys in there and begin playing.

When my children were younger, people would often comment on how good they were at packing up after themselves. They'd ask what I bribed them with or say it must have been the child's organised personality. But the truth is, although I did teach them to pack up and they are organised children, I attribute the bulk of this habit to two things. Firstly, how many toys we had in the home – and secondly, how they were organised to begin with.

The more toys you own, the more effort is required to keep them organised. Keeping the toys in your home to a reasonable amount gives your children the freedom to enjoy what they have without you feeling the burden of constantly needing to tidy up.

When children can see clearly where things are to be packed up, they'll learn to pack up after themselves. If the whole room looks like a toy shop after an earthquake they're probably not going to know where anything goes.

Children learn through example and repetition, so in the beginning your partner or you will be doing the packing up yourself. But you'll have a little person alongside you, watching how Mummy or Daddy does it. You teach them as you go – 'blocks go all together in this container and dolls go in this other box with a picture of a dolly on it. See how there is a picture of food on this box? Well, that's where all the play food from the kitchen goes.'

2. Toys

I did a teaching course many years ago and the one thing I remember is that to teach someone something, you go through a process:

1. I show you
2. You help me
3. You do it
4. You show someone else

My own experience tells me if you follow these steps with a child, soon you'll have a little someone who understands how to pack up after themselves. The fourth step can be showing a grandparent when they visit how well they can pack up, or teaching a younger sibling or friend who comes to play. I wish I had a magic wand that meant you didn't have to ask them to pack up (sometimes multiple times), but if you make packing up correctly a non-negotiable task in your family, your children will be equipped to integrate this skill into all areas of their lives.

When I talk about toys, don't just think of the toy box in the family room. Also think of toys that live in bedrooms or toys that have made their way into your car. Toys can be found in the bathroom (bath toys), rumpus or toy room, even in the garage if you ran out of room inside the house.

When it comes to organising toys, some parents choose to do this in full stealth mode. They wait until their unassuming children are fast asleep or at a sleepover, then they do a big toy cull. Toys destined for the op-shop are hidden in the boot of the car, covered by an old picnic rug to shield from roaming eyes. Broken toys (and admittedly sometimes really annoying toys, like the plastic recorder that was a gift from their favourite uncle) are stuffed deep down in the outside rubbish bin.

They wait with baited breath when the kids wake up or come home, fingers crossed they don't notice that anything is missing. Parents claim innocence when a child is searching for their 'favourite' toy. Maybe they'll keep looking and you'll have five minutes of peace! I mean, that's what some parents do … other parents of course, but not us.

Believe it or not, there are ways to help your child declutter their own toys without causing a monumental meltdown. I have parents hire me to work with their children and I've always had great success, partly because I'm not their parent, and partly because I'm helping them develop routines and teaching the philosophy behind tidying, instead of nagging for the job to be done.

First step is to gather all the toys in your home into one room. This might seem daunting at first, but get the kids to help by going room to room and bringing everything out onto the floor of a large communal area. If your living room isn't big enough to do this, you could use the garage if you have one. Do a quick check of the house (all the places I listed above that may have toys inside) and make sure you have everything (check the bottom of wardrobes and under beds!).

First step is to group all the toys into categories. For example:

- Puzzles
- Board games
- Make-believe toys (shopping, kitchen, prams, etc.)
- Dress-ups
- Building blocks/Lego
- Dolls and teddies
- Arts and crafts

- Sports equipment
- Puppets
- Instruments
- Dinosaurs
- Toy cars
- Magic sets

Your family will have different categories than mine, but see how things naturally group around what your child plays with.

Once you've made these groups on the floor you can quickly see which toys are broken or missing pieces and no longer work. These can go straight into the bin. Something I used to say to my kids when they got upset that a toy broke and needed to be thrown out was, 'When a toy breaks from playing with it so much, that's a good thing. It means you loved it and played with it a lot. Toys aren't meant to last forever – think of all the fun you had playing with it.'

Once broken toys are thrown out, you can ask your children to pick out anything that they've outgrown or don't play with anymore. Get them to make quick decisions and encourage them to be realistic about what they still play with. They may select toys that surprise you, but if you're prepared to go with what they say I'd suggest not putting back toys they are happy to declutter.

These toys will go one of two places: you can donate them or sell them. If they pull out toys that cost you a lot of money, you may consider selling these online if you're not comfortable with donating them. Use a large container or box to put these two categories of toys in ('sell' and 'donate'), to be handled at the end of the day. I suggest keeping them out of the children's sight once decided upon, because if they're left in the family room things will start disappearing from the container and make their way back into the toy collection.

Take the donate box to the op-shop as soon as you can. Clients have often told me that it wasn't until the donations were dropped off did they truly feel like the decluttering was complete. List the toys online as soon as you can and give yourself a limit to how long you'll keep them while trying to sell them. You might decide that whatever is still unsold at the end of the week gets donated.

(Parent Note: at some point during the toy decluttering your child will pick up a toy that a grandparent gave them, saying they don't like it and want to donate it. Resist guilt-tripping your child into keeping it 'so that Nanna doesn't get upset'. Teach your children healthy relationships with possessions by allowing them to dislike a gift while still respecting and honouring the gift-giver – more on that later!)

What's left should be a (probably larger than you imagined) collection of toys that your children use and want to keep. Now that you've decluttered, it's time to organise what's left.

I have found that regardless of the size or style of family, toys are always best kept in containers. Containers make packing up easy, storage easy and also make play easy when a child is looking for a particular item.

My suggestion is to use a separate container for each category of toys. I've always kept two different sized containers for toys as some only need a small space, while things like dress-ups can take up a larger space. Containers without clip locks are best for children so you don't need to open it up every time they want something. If you can find containers on wheels this is also great, as toys can be moved from room to room easily.

If you buy large containers, consider that your children may not be able to reach to the bottom or may pull it on top of themselves while trying to get toys out. Smaller sized containers seem to work best for children of all ages. Something that they can use when they're little and something they can carry when they're a bit older.

I'm big into labelling all toy boxes and containers. Without labels children will just throw everything in together, but with labels they can quickly and easily know what goes where. If your child isn't old enough to read, a picture of what goes inside the container works well. In my experience, children as young as eighteen months old learn quickly which toys go where and will happily correct you if you put something in the wrong box! Labels are also temporary enough that when your child outgrows a particular toy, you can relabel it for whatever it is they're playing with now (then donate or sell the toys they've grown out of).

I've got a special relationship with my label maker – she (yes, it's a girl labeller) makes my life easier. When my kids were little friends used to laugh at how every single storage box was labelled. Then it came time for the kids to pack up; they'd watch as one and three year olds quickly (and happily!) put things away where they belonged. It's a habit that's continued as they've got older, and I'm happy to report they still now like keeping their rooms organised.

How to decide where to keep these containers of toys … all in one place or some in each room? My personal preference, and one I've seen work well for most clients, is to have the majority of toys kept together in the one space. Depending on your family preferences, it could be the kids bedrooms, a playroom, toy room, rumpus or family living area. Whatever you choose, keeping all the containers together means you always know where something is, always know where to put it away and your home doesn't become cluttered with toys in every room.

You may wish to just have containers that stack, or a storage unit that containers can fit inside to further hide the toys away. I have a combination of both. And when the kids are little and have big toys (a shop, ride-on toys, a cubby, table and chairs, rocking horse, etc.) these can be kept in the same space, but understandably not hidden from view. We're not trying to pretend children don't live in our homes – we're just working toward our home not being overtaken by toys and toys not dominating all our living spaces.

'But I have a two storey house and need toys on both levels.'

Then I would recommend having containers that live upstairs for the most part, and some that for the most part live downstairs. Carrying boxes of toys and up and down stairs isn't the safest option, so have dedicated toys on each level to minimise transportation.

Having toys kept in containers has the added benefit of keeping them in better condition than if they were all in a tub in the playroom:

- Puzzle and game pieces are less likely to be lost.
- Dolls' clothing and accessories are kept in the same place as the dolls.
- Sets of toys can be played with by groups of children, as they are all kept together.
- Soft toys can be quickly gathered and washed if they get dusty.
- Paints, arts and crafts are contained so they don't dry out or spread mess.

If your child no longer plays with their playdough, for example, you can grab the whole container with tubs of playdough, rolling pins, shape cutters, etc., and sell the lot quickly online or bag them up for donation.

2. Toys

I know that you'll find your home more organised by being intentional about decluttering and organising your children's toys. It's also less confronting than starting with your heirlooms or clothing (much easier to declutter things for someone else than for yourself!)

Simple Tips

- Work alongside your children to declutter toys they don't play with anymore. Ask them to donate anything they don't use, don't play with or don't like anymore.

- Buy child-friendly sized containers for your children's toys and put each category of toys in a separate, clearly labelled box.

- Talk with your family about where the best places to keep toys are in your home.

Kitchen

'There's nothing to eat!'

*I*s there anything more frustrating than getting home from the supermarket, having spent $200 on groceries and feeling like there is still nothing in the house to eat?

Venture with me through this chapter to learn how you can organise and declutter your kitchen in just one afternoon.

Having an organised kitchen will save you money each week at the supermarket (I'll explain how I saved $1000 in just one month). You'll find that you're eating healthier and feeling inspired to cook yummy meals for yourself and your family, instead of reverting to take-away when you can't decide what to cook.

Food prices have increased so much over the past decade that we can't afford to continue throwing out food at our current rate.

Australians discard up to 20% of the food they purchase.[1] Imagine that for every five bags of groceries you buy, one full bag goes straight into the bin.

A disorganised kitchen and pantry leads to a general aversion to spending unnecessary time in your kitchen each day. This will result in wasted food, wasted money and unhealthy eating habits. None of which we can afford as busy women.

Food

Food can be stored in many places in your kitchen/home. The obvious places are your pantry and fridge/freezer, but you may also have a larder for cans/tins and bulk purchases. Many people now have a deep freezer and most Australian homes have at least two fridges (the second fridge is usually the drinks fridge). I won't get started on how much it costs to run a second fridge, but if you're trying to cut down your electricity bill, turn it off for a couple of months and see the difference.

A few years ago, after noticing how much food clients were throwing out, I decided to set our family a challenge. We call it 'Eat Yourself Out of House and Home'.

For the month of June each year we now attempt to use up everything in our pantry, fridge and freezer. We do this to reduce food wastage, using food before it eventually goes off. Herbs, spices, tins, jars, frozen meat, condiments – all have use-by dates and if they're only used a few times, you'll probably end up throwing the majority of it away.

---

1. 'Fast Facts on Food Waste', Foodwise, <http://www.foodwise.com.au/foodwaste/food-waste-fast-facts/>

So instead of having things go off, we aim to use up each item we've already purchased. During the month we still purchase fresh fruit and veggies, bread, milk and dairy products, but the bulk of our groceries are things we already have in the kitchen.

If you own a deep freezer (or even a normal freezer) you'll know the trick of making a double batch of casserole or soup, freeze half and then twelve months later you have no idea what it is or how long it's been there for, so you throw it away. In this way, instead of saving you money, the freezer ends up costing you money to store then throw out food that was perfectly good to begin with, but now ends up in the bin.

Just a side note on freezers – I've started freezing everything in clear containers with clear lids. That way, I can always tell what's inside. Since doing this, not one thing has been wasted in our freezer. I've now got several clients doing the same and they love it. It also means everything can stack easily, which increases the space in the freezer and makes it easy to find something that you're looking for.

One June when our family did the 'Eat Yourself Out of House and Home' challenge, we kept a note of how much we saved compared to our usual monthly grocery bill. The result was shocking (in a good way).

Over the month of June we saved a massive $1000 in thirty days. This even included food for my birthday and a weekend away. At the end our pantry, fridge and freezer were almost completely empty. It was a great feeling; we'd saved so much money but we'd also avoided having to throw out food that would have otherwise gone off.

I should probably admit that we did have to throw out three bottles of marinade that I'd purchased on sale (!) but hadn't used and they'd gone off. But I reckon that's not too bad in the scheme of things.

I love it when people do their own 'Eat Yourself Out of House and Home' challenge. It's fun to hear what new recipes people came up with, what they found at the back of the freezer and how much money they saved. I found some really yummy baking recipes by putting a few ingredients into Google and seeing what I could find. We discovered coconut flour, almond meal and dark chocolate chip biscuits that were amazing. We also have a gluten-free coconut cake that was so easy I've made it many times since.

Another tip to reducing food waste is to keep your pantry items in clear containers. Regardless of the brand you choose, sticking with one type is important so it stacks and fits nicely. This way you'll avoid food spoiling when you only use half a packet of something. It's also handy for when you do your shopping list because you won't double up on items you already have, and you can see everything clearly.

(Simple Tip: label every container even if you think you'll remember what is inside – we've all heard stories of sugar and salt being mixed up or bicarb soda being used instead of icing sugar!)

'We shop in bulk so our pantry is always full.'

Buying in bulk is excellent for saving money – but only if you actually use what you buy. If you buy in bulk but end up throwing out some of what you buy, you're also throwing out your savings. So make sure you run out of an item before purchasing it again in bulk. Alternatively you could do bulk purchasing with a neighbour and share the savings without bringing dozens of cans or kilos of meat into your kitchen in one go.

> ***If you buy in bulk but end up throwing out some of what you buy, you're also throwing out your savings.***

So whether you choose to take on the 'Eat Yourself Out of House and Home' challenge or not, decluttering your pantry then organising what you have left will save you money, no matter which way you look at it.

Kitchen

The kitchen is one of my favourite rooms in the house to help clients organise, because we can make such a big difference in just one afternoon. Your kitchen is probably the most used room in your home, and is called the heart of the home for a reason. We all love to gather around food, around kitchen benches and at friends' tables. Food brings people together from all walks of life, so it's important to have a safe, functional and clean kitchen in your home.

The kitchen also has high demands put on it: its storage is always full, traffic is high and both accessibility and functionality are crucial. So stop for a minute and think about the things you keep in your kitchen:

- Crockery
- Cutlery
- Utensils
- Tableware

- Drinking glasses
- Wine glasses
- Coffee cups
- Appliances
- Servingware
- Platters
- Bakeware
- Plastics
- Knife set

And each category listed above can be decluttered to make it easier to move around and use your kitchen space. I can't go through everything here, so I'll focus on a few.

Firstly – crockery. This one can make a big difference quickly. I want you to take out every single piece of crockery you own and place it on the kitchen table. Don't worry about serving dishes or salad bowls – we're talking about dinner plates, bowls, side plates, pasta bowls, noodle bowls and anything else you eat out of.

First thing to do is to donate any 'crockery orphans'. If you started off with a full crockery set for four, but along the way half have broken, then the rest are orphans and can be donated.

For some of you, mismatched sets make you happy so go for it. If you prefer matching, keep reading.

You can pick up inexpensive dinner sets from Kmart, Big W or Ikea so replacing orphaned sets with a matching set isn't going to cost you a lot of money. Many clients find they don't actually have a full set of crockery, even though they have enough to get them by day to day.

My suggestion is to buy a matching set of crockery that can serve twelve, and get rid of everything else. This looks good visually, but has other benefits too.

Having just one style of crockery makes stacking the dishwasher easier, makes putting dishes away easier, makes setting the table easier … and anything that makes all those things easier in my book is a winner!

Gone are the days where families needed to have a 'good set' of crockery for dinner parties. If you have a matching set of twelve, you can then use them for everyday family meals as well as special occasions. And as pieces break over time (which is inevitable) you can just buy replacement pieces or sets to match what you already have.

Here's the nitty gritty of what I keep in my crockery drawer … twelve dinner plates, twelve side plates, twelve soup bowls and twelve noodle bowls. We are a family of four, but often will have 10–12 around the dinner table when friends visit.

I've never run out and I still feel like it's a minimal amount to keep. If we did have more than twelve for a meal, we could quickly pull out our picnic set, which has plastic bowls and plates in it, to use for the kids.

'I can't just throw things out because they don't match.'

Yes you can! I give you permission to buy a new set of crockery (you'll be able to buy enough for twelve people for under $100) and to throw out your old mismatched pieces.

These are items that you'll use 3–4 times every day, so get something nice and matching and you'll find your kitchen runs that bit easier.

Next, have a think about your glassware. Do you have enough glasses if you have twelve people for lunch? Do your glasses fit in your dishwasher easily? Do you enjoy drinking from them?

Almost all clients that I work with have a collection of mismatched glasses in their kitchen. Three in one style, a set of six in another, one random glass yet to break from another set.

Just like with crockery, make life easier for yourself and buy a large set of glasses in a style, size and price range that you like. Glasses break (which is probably why you have so many orphans in the glass cupboard) and when you buy new ones, few people give thought to getting ones to match what they already have.

I personally have twenty-four matching glasses in our cupboard. When people come over they'll often use one glass while we eat nibbles and another glass will be set at the table. We have twelve matching wine glasses that make setting a matching table super-easy.

Another area I want to dive deeper into is that of your kitchen appliances. I've seen so many (mostly unused) kitchen appliances hidden away at the back of cupboards around the country. Appliances that can boil six eggs at once, pie makers, donut makers, coffee machines, blenders, food processors, milkshake makers, yoghurt makers, grinders, slushie makers, urns, sushi makers, juicers, ice cream makers … the list goes on!

What I've noticed is that 90% of these appliances never get used. Some were received as gifts or purchased at the sales, but they get pushed to the back of the cupboard – out of sight and out of mind.

3. Kitchen

So, I'm sure you've worked out what I want you to do next. That's right – get every single kitchen appliance you own and set them up on the bench. If you own a Thermomix or similar product, I want you to pop that on the bench too.

You have permission to leave your kettle and toaster plugged in, because I'm yet to meet a family who doesn't need those two items. But if you have a 'spare' toaster or kettle they need to be out on the bench.

First thing is to throw out anything that is broken or missing parts required to work. For me, I need to throw out our electric knife as it is fifteen years old and the blades are locked in the handle, so we can't take them out to clean them after use. I'm not sure how much it will be to replace it, but after fifteen years and carving many a yummy roast and homemade loaf of bread, it has served its time.

Next, if you have two things that do the same job, pick one to keep and one to donate. Two food processors? Donate the smaller one. Two juicers? Donate the one that's harder to use. You get the idea.

The next obvious group is appliances that you own, but never or rarely use. These are often novelty items like a pie maker, which you may have used once when you got it, but you're not a pie-making kind of person so no need to keep it. Same for things like an ice cream maker – good in theory, but how many times have you actually used it? If you do, then of course keep it!

Side note on appliances – if you've purchased an all-in-one machine like a Thermomix, then don't keep smaller appliances that do the same jobs. No need to keep a rice cooker or food processor if you can do it in a multi-function machine.

Once you're down to the appliances you do and will use, keep them in easy reach. Don't stash them away at the back of a cupboard; you'll forget you even have them. If you have space, keep them in the pantry or in a cupboard you can easily reach. Make it easier to use them than for you to manually do their job.

If you've decluttered your crockery, glassware and appliances and feel ready to get into the rest of your kitchenware, at some stage you'll probably find yourself saying, 'We might need these for when we throw parties.' I'd encourage you to ask yourself a couple of questions before you decide to keep six salad bowls and a dozen white platters.

1. When was the last time I threw a party and needed all these items?
2. If I did need more serving dishes than I own, could I borrow them from a friend, family member or neighbour?

Deciding what to keep is as individual as every family, but asking yourself some helpful questions will make the process easier. If you're getting stuck, put items you're not sure you'll need in a box in the garage (or under a bed as a friend did) and see which items you need to retrieve over the next six months. Whatever is left in there after your set amount of time can be taken straight to the op-shop.

And can you do me a little favour … as you're taking things out of the cupboards to declutter them, give the cupboards a wipe over before you start putting things back in. You'll be glad you did and perhaps a little shocked as to how dirty they can get over the years.

3. Kitchen

Simple Tips

- Practice the habit of eating what you have in the house before purchasing more food. Join me for June's 'eat yourself out of house and home month'.

- Donate any crockery orphans and purchase a matching set of twelve for everyday use.

- Get all your appliances in one place and keep only those that you love and use.

Wardrobe

'It still has the tags on.'

There is a universal guilt we feel when we see clothes in our wardrobe that still have their tags on. But it often doesn't stop us hitting the sales, picking up a bargain or buying something we like, even if we can't imagine where we'll wear it.

But the guilt is real. It's a mixture of regret, embarrassment and indecision. It's regret that you purchased it in the first place (you can still see on that tag how much it cost you). It's embarrassment that you've done it again – you've purchased something, never worn it and left it idly taking up space in your wardrobe. And the indecision is around 'shoulds'. *I should sell it. I should donate it. I should wear it.* Indecision is paralysing and the benefit of working with a professional organiser is that they help you process the decisions, taking away the power of indecision and the stagnant place where it leaves you.

Having a decluttered and organised wardrobe will make it easier to get dressed in the morning – you'll love everything you own and can see what you have. You'll find that you always look good – clothes that weren't flattering are gone and what's left is a wardrobe full of clothes that suit your personality and style.

It is so much easier to put washing away when your wardrobe is organised. Instead of clean clothes sitting in a washing basket for days, it can take two minutes and it's all away. It's such a great feeling to know that there isn't any washing sitting around, needing to be put away!

And let's talk about the money side of your wardrobe. Being organised means you're less likely to spend unnecessary money on items you don't really need. And any clothes that you donate from your current wardrobe will go towards supporting charities and someone will love the items you donate.

It's estimated that women in Australia wear only 20% of their clothes. That's a lot of space being taken up by items you don't like, don't wear or that don't fit you anymore.

You know the feeling of having nothing to wear despite having hundreds of items of clothing? Well, if you choose to do nothing about it, that's exactly how it's going to stay.

I'm not saying it will be easy. Lots of women find going through their clothes confronting and quite emotional. If your weight has changed, admitting that clothes don't fit anymore can be really difficult. If you really wanted another baby but haven't been able to fall pregnant, decluttering maternity wear can stir feelings of grief. If your wedding dress has lasted longer than the marriage it's hard to close a chapter of your life by letting go of it.

If your self-confidence has taken a battering and you never feel nice in what you wear, it's so hard to pick items that you want to keep, because everything in your wardrobe reminds you that you don't feel good enough.

I find it such a privilege to work alongside women through this process. I love looking in their eyes and telling them that they're beautiful regardless of what they wear. After all, the fashion industry does not define your beauty or your value. And through a process (and often tears) we decide what she loves and what she feels comfortable in, to organise this very intimate and practical part of a woman's life.

You may think, 'But it's just clothes, what's the big deal?' but I speak from experience in saying that what may look like just organising a wardrobe will often reveal your innermost feelings about yourself. This can be a really healing process to go through with someone.

> *The fashion industry does not define your beauty or your value.*

My rule when it comes to your clothes is: eliminate first – organise second.

So before we start pulling everything out of the wardrobe, there's a step you need to do a few days in advance. Get up to date on the washing. It's very hard to know what you have when most of the 20% that you actually wear is on the line or sitting in a laundry hamper. So once everything is washed and dried you're ready to start.

First things first: make your bed! Sounds silly, but piling clothes on an unmade bed makes everything harder. It's harder to see what clothes you have when they're mixed in with sheets – and the reward of finishing is also dampened when the wardrobe now looks amazing and the bed sits there unmade. Once your bed is made, it's time to start decluttering.

Any clothes that are ripped, stained, have shrunk or stretched are thrown out straight away. This goes for shoes that have seen better days too. Stockings with runs, socks with holes and lingerie that has lost its elasticity – all go in the bin.

Now grab a bag for donations. I want you to quickly pick ten items that you know you don't wear and can be donated straight away. Try to take less than one minute to pick these ten items. These will be the items you don't even need to think about – you know that you don't like them, they don't fit, etc.

Now that those two quick steps are done it's time to go through your clothes, category by category. This is where the made bed and having the laundry up to date will really help. Lay every single item you have in that category on the bed. This is crunch time. How many do you need? What do you like to wear? Are there any that don't fit anymore? As you ask these questions, some things will go in the donation bag and others will become your keep pile.

Some category suggestions are:

- Jackets
- Jumpers/hoodies
- Cardigans
- Jeans
- Pants

- Skirts
- Suits
- Singlet tops
- T-shirts
- Long sleeve tops
- Dresses (casual)
- Dresses (formal)
- Shorts
- Leggings
- Active wear
- Swimwear
- Undies/bras
- Socks and stockings
- Shoes
- Sleepwear
- Scarves and gloves
- Work uniforms

You may have even more categories than that, but as you can see we're being quite specific. Rather than just getting all your tops out, do your singlet tops first, then your t-shirts, then long sleeve tops.

I have to admit that I have a little bit of a singlet top obsession. I wear them underneath almost every outfit. I wear them in summer and winter – I find them so comfortable and great for layering. I have about five black singlet tops alone, but because I wear them so often I'm keeping them all. Your thing might be dresses and you wear them all the time, so keep the ones you love.

There isn't some magic number of items of clothes you're allowed to keep. My suggestion is to be fully present when deciding what to keep. Hold each item and decide if you love it. If you're being honest with yourself throughout the process, your donate pile will probably be much larger than you imagined. Don't get stuck on thinking how much money you spent on those clothes, but rather see the end goal; that your wardrobe will now be full of clothes you love and have enough space to store things well.

'I love this top; if I lose 5kg it will fit again, I'm sure.'

My suggestion is that if you want to keep something as a goal top to fit back into, then keep just the one item in that size and try it on every month or so to see how you're going. But keeping half a wardrobe of clothes that are a size or two too small is only going to make you feel discouraged. If you do reach a size goal, treat yourself to some new clothes that are in season and reflect your new body shape well.

'That dress cost me $150, I really should try to sell it.'

Sure thing – give it a go. But place a limit on how long you'll keep it while trying to sell it. My recommendation is to give it 2 weeks. If it hasn't sold in 2 weeks, give it away. You'll never make back the full amount you spent on it so sometimes, for the headspace it occupies, it's better to let it go.

Now, I know that every family is different, every wardrobe is different, every bedroom is different – so the following is purely what I've found to work best in my home and in the homes of clients. Have a listen to how I do things and see if you think it might work for you.

4. Wardrobe

This is a quick summary of how I store clothes.

- All tops are hung up. This includes t-shirts, singlet tops, jumpers, jackets and long sleeve tops. This way nothing gets squashed at the back of a drawer and you can quickly see everything you have. (It's also much easier to put them away.)
- I hang all jeans/pants so I can easily see what I have.
- I use basket drawers (mesh ones so they breathe) for anything that doesn't need to be kept wrinkle-free. In these drawers I don't try to keep them organised beyond only keeping what belongs in there together. I'm not someone who folds my undies or keeps my bras in colour order. I value efficiency above perfection so that's how I organise my clothes. The drawers are as follows:
    - Sleepwear, all in together like a happy family (tops, pants, shorts, etc.)
    - Shorts
    - Socks and stockings
    - Bathers (also keep my goggles, swimming cap and sarong in here too)
    - Bras
    - Leggings
    - Active wear
    - Work uniforms (mine don't need to be hung, so they all just go in here)
    - Beanies, gloves and headbands

You get the idea – like goes with like, so things are easy to find and more importantly, easy to put away.

Are you someone who dumps their clothes on a chair or on the floor at night rather than put them away? I totally used to do that. It was a mixture of lazy ('It's clean so I'll just wear it again tomorrow'), and it was too difficult to put things away all the time because the wardrobe was already busting at the seams.

My friend's mum has a saying that I now repeat to my clients: 'You're going to have to put it away at some stage, so it might as well be now.' She also had a good tip when it came to the clothes that had another wear left in them (a suit jacket, jumper, jeans, etc.) that instead of putting them in the 'not quite dirty or not quite clean' pile in your bedroom she'd say, 'If they're clean enough to wear again, they're clean enough enough to hang up.' Makes total sense, but how many of us have a jumper that seems to never be hung up because 'I'll wear it again soon'?

Give yourself a whole afternoon or evening and you'll be able to get your wardrobe completely organised. Having an honest friend around to help will make the process more enjoyable too.

If you've got to this stage, then well done! You'll be feeling lighter already. Make sure you drop the donation bags off to charity so they don't sit around the house for weeks driving you crazy (speaking from experience!).

Last hurdle: what if you genuinely don't have enough space in your wardrobe for what you've decided to keep? Rental properties often have the bare minimum of one shelf and a hanging rail installed, and if you own your own home you might think you need to spend thousands to get a custom-built internal wardrobe. Not so. I mean, if you have the cash sitting around, go for it – you'll love it. But if you'd prefer to go with a less expensive option I have a few suggestions.

One option is to purchase a stand-alone, click-together wardrobe system to either keep inside your current wardrobe space or in a bedroom. These can be quite inexpensive and functionally fantastic, but they're not pretty. A chest of drawers will look much nicer and can be a great way to store things that don't need to be hung.

Another option (particularly good for children) is to purchase a cube storage unit that will fit in the bottom of their wardrobe. Use the fabric containers to keep things like school uniforms, sports uniforms, swimwear, sleepwear, etc.

The biggest tip I can give you in regards to keeping your wardrobe organised is this: donate what you don't wear and put away what you do.

Simple Tips

- Gather all your items of clothes from around the house (think coats, washing, shoes at back door, etc.) and put them all together so you can see what you have.
- Donate anything you don't love or doesn't fit anymore.
- Organise your clothes in a way that's easy to put things away and easy to find what you're looking for.

Organised Car

My 1997 Ford Falcon was my first 'adult' car because it was younger than I was. It had electric windows at the front, rear speakers and I even got a CD player installed. I never ran out of petrol, never blew a tyre and I never fixed a dent after an accident. It wasn't a bomb ... it was well loved. I brought both our kids home from hospital in the backseat (and nearly delivered baby number two in the front seat!) and it was a reliable car. Since then I've bought a new car and it's luxurious in comparison.

I don't like letting the petrol get too low, I get my car serviced regularly and in the day I'm sure our child restraints were the best fitted in Australia. I don't use my car as a dumping ground. There are no coffee cups in the cup holders and no apple cores in the backseat. It's not super clean but it's organised (story of my life). And I like to be prepared.

As well as having a boot full of storage containers for clients, I'm prepared for other situations should they arise. Here's the inside scoop on how you too can keep your car organised.

The first thing every car needs is a first aid kit. Mine isn't huge or flashy but it has a couple of bandages, *lots* of rubber gloves (have never had to use them at the scene of an accident, but a 'number two' explosion from a child required their use many years ago), Band-Aids, antibacterial swabs, tweezers … you get the idea. My first aid kit is kept in the glove compartment.

My mum bought me a torch for the car when I first got my licence. She thought it would keep me safe if I ever broke down in the bush at night. I used it once … as a microphone while singing along to John Farnham.

In the glove box is also a roll of gaffer tape (which fixes everything!), my service history and the car manual so I know important things like how to reprogram the Bluetooth should it ever stop working.

I always keep spare change in the ashtray (are they even called that anymore?) in case I need milk on the way home from the gym or need to pay for parking. Wipes and tissues live in the console along with a stash of McDonald's serviettes for emergencies.

We spend a lot of our time in our cars, so might as well be organised in there too.

Housework

'I'm out of clean socks.'

I debated whether to include this chapter or not ... housework and routines are hardly a sexy topic!

I do have to state from the start that I'm not talking about cleaning tips or how to get your toilet to shine – I'm going to be talking about chores and how getting organised in this area of life will give you back time, headspace and even money.

If you feel like your list of chores is always too long, and you dream of Mary Poppins coming to visit, this chapter is for you! If you've never had birds turn up to sing with you when you're tidying the family room or children dancing around their bedrooms cleaning up, then I'm your girl.

Sometimes I relate more to Mrs Banks (the mother of the house in *Mary Poppins*). She's a working mother with a husband who works a highly demanding job. She has two children she adores, but also feels overwhelmed trying to parent at times. And then along comes Mary Poppins – her nanny in shining armour. Mary Poppins is 'perfect in every way', which really just points out that Mrs Banks is not (poor Mrs Banks).

My aim is to take you from a stressed out, overburdened Mrs Banks and move you closer toward a Mary Poppins. Not all the way – just a few steps closer. A few realistic, achievable steps closer to her motto of: 'In every job that must be done, there is an element of fun.'

I'll talk about how my house is always 'pop-in friendly' and how my family works together to keep our home running smoothly. It's about helping you find your groove and being flexible enough that when life throws curve balls, you don't end up throwing in the (slightly off-smelling, should have been washed yesterday) towel.

Every single home in the world has chores that need to be done. And if you don't do them, chances are you'll end up on a reality TV show where they find dead rodents in your kitchen, and you're filmed saying things like, 'I haven't been inside that room for five years, I'm not even sure what's in there.' Don't be that family!

Because you've got this far, I know you want to manage your home well and reduce stress, frustration and guilt – but we're not aiming to win any superwoman awards. My aim is to achieve efficiency, not perfection. And that's key when it comes to routines around the home.

Firstly, let me address my statement that my home is always 'pop-in friendly'.

This doesn't mean it's always perfectly clean and tidy. Far from it. It means that it's always more important to me to have friends and family over than it is to live in a display home. One of my friends shared a great article the other day on 'messy hospitality'. I loved it – the concept was that in order to live life with people, sometimes we have to do messy hospitality.

Don't put off having people over because you're in a mess. Don't suggest meeting at a café just because your washing is over the heating vents and your sink is full of dishes. Instead, allow people to love you for who you are and love them back accordingly. I want to dispel the myth that being an organised housewife means having your home in a constantly perfect state.

Some of my friends are perfectionists when it comes to their homes. And if that's you, go for it. Wash the floors every day, strip the beds and change the sheets twice a week – if that's what floats your boat, don't let me rain on your parade.

My clients will tell you that I have a little motto when it comes to keeping the house organised: 'Fifteen minutes from perfection *is* perfect.' If you can get your home completely organised in fifteen minutes, then that's a win. For me, that means putting throws/pillows where they belong (and not on the floor where my children think they belong).

It means having the kitchen table clear and the kitchen bench clear. It means that toys lying around can be packed up and things can be returned to their correct places. The load of washing on the couch can be put away, remotes returned to where they belong and random socks on the floor are in the wash (tell me it isn't just my family that always has socks on the ground!)

Now, I'm not expecting that you're there already. The fifteen minutes from perfection is where I aim to have my clients after they're finished working with me. We're not running display homes, but we're not living in chaos either.

Let me give you a recent example – a few months ago I received a call from a journalist at Channel 9, asking if she could interview me for a story about organising.

It was 9 am on a Thursday morning and I'd just dropped off the boys at school. They said they'd be at my home in an hour. I looked around the house and wanted it to be a great advert for my business so I knew it would be a busy hour. I needed to do a fifteen minute tidy, followed by fifteen minutes of cleaning, followed by fifteen minutes of getting myself ready (gotta have good hair if you're going to be on TV!) and then fifteen minutes to 'style' my house for the shoot.

The timer was on and I got to work. I rang my sister who is good at styling (not my forte) and she arrived in time to help me style and pick what I was going to wear. Before she arrived I tidied every room in the house in fifteen minutes. Nothing on the floors, beds made, toys away, flat surfaces clear, desk tidy, etc. Fifteen minutes for the whole house – four bedrooms, kitchen, living room and two studies.

The only reason this was even possible is because I'm an organised person and I like to keep the house clutter-free. And this can be you too – stick with me and I'll show you how. I got everything tidied, cleaned (quick once-over in the bathrooms and kitchen), dressed and styled before they arrived.

The interview was a huge success and a great reinforcement that fifteen minutes from perfection is indeed perfect!

When my friends and family are popping over, I don't aim for perfection. I just aim for organised. My friends don't come over to inspect my house, and neither will yours. But it is important to me to feel like my home is welcoming, not cluttered and that it's relaxing. I like that there won't be toys in the living room and towels on the bathroom floor. I like that if your child grazes their knee I know where the Band-Aids are. That's my desire and that's why I do it, not to impress anyone else.

> *We're not running display homes, but we're not living in chaos either.*

My aim is to help you think about ways to streamline your household chores and routines. Ways to reduce stress. I've provided some tips that have helped me and helped my clients.

So in this chapter, I'm going to give you a few hot tips on ways to save time, headspace and money with household routines.

Washing

I start with washing because it's actually my favourite household chore. I find it relaxing. I like the feeling of being on top of the washing and I hang the washing out just how I like it, so it dries quickly and is easy to put away when I bring it inside. I like the quiet of being out at the line; it's space to think and it's me time.

Now don't get your feminist knickers in a knot – I'm not saying anything more than I personally enjoy doing the washing. Not suggesting you should like it; not suggesting it's a woman's job. Just saying for me it's time out to think, reflect and enjoy feeling productive.

First hot tip for washing: never have dirty clothes hampers in children's bedrooms. Why? Because even if an item of clothing has only been worn for half an hour, it's easier for an eight year old to chuck it in the hamper than return it to the wardrobe. You'll end up washing clean clothes, and none of us have the time for that!

Set a load of washing to go before you head to bed at night. Set a delay so clothes won't sit wet in the machine all night, but instead finish just before you get up in the morning. This way, whoever in your house hangs the washing out can do it before heading to work or school. It also means that you don't spend your weekend pumping out five loads of washing, because you've been able to keep on top of it during the week.

I'm constantly amazed at how many homes have a spare room with baskets full of clean washing. Biggest I've seen was a double bed piled at least a metre high with clean clothes just waiting to be put away. We addressed part of the problem in the previous chapter – we have too many clothes, so not only does putting them away become difficult due to lack of space, but we have so many clothes we don't miss those not yet put away. Being on top of the washing will reduce the number of items you 'need', therefore saving you money.

My hot tip is to put washing away as soon as you bring it in. Make it one single process if you can. Bring the basket in, and then go room to room putting it away straight from the basket. This will also mean clothes are less creased, which is great if you don't like ironing.

Once my boys hit primary school they became responsible for putting their own washing away (most of the time!). So to streamline this, I use three different baskets for clean washing. One for each child and then one for my husband and me. These get popped on their beds so when they get home from school, they can put everything away and return the basket to the laundry.

If you're in the habit of leaving clean washing sitting around, this is a habit that you can change – if you do, it will make your chores seem less cumbersome as you won't feel like you're constantly looking at a job that needs to be done.

Changing Sheets and Towels

If I lived on my own, had endless time and energy and less concern for the environment then I would change my bath towels every single day. I love clean towels so much – but changing them every day doesn't match my values, so I restrain. And with bedsheets, unless a child has had an accident or you've got particular reason to change them, weekly or fortnightly is totally fine. I'm not the housework police – my aim is to help you streamline whatever schedule works for your family.

Having a routine for these simple chores does make my life easier. And hopefully it will make your life easier if you choose to do it too.

For bedsheets, my aim is to wash them and return them to the bed the same day. I'm yet to meet anyone who loves folding bedsheets, especially Queen or King size, so I avoid folding them by washing, drying and returning them to the bed as quickly as possible.

On a typical washing day, for instance … before the boys leave for school I ask them to strip their beds and put their sheets in the washing machine. I put a load of sheets straight on, and then once they're washed I hang them out (or put them through the dryer if it's raining). By dinner time they're sitting back on the boys' beds, ready for them to make the bed that night. Yes, my primary school aged boys know how to strip their beds and make them. (They're not in bunks so it's not rocket science.)

If you're out of the home during the day, this can easily be done on a weekend – or when it's warm or windy enough, you can hang them out before work and have them in before bedtime. Whatever routine works for your family, but gotta say I don't miss folding sheets every week.

Rubbish

I've just got one hot tip to give you around taking advantage of rubbish day. On bin night once all the regular bins have been emptied, grab a bag (or give the kids a bag each) and spend two minutes walking around the house, collecting any rubbish that hasn't made it into a bin.

We do this every week and I'm amazed how easily we fill a bag. Things like invites on the fridge for events passed, craft that was displayed but can now be taken down, junk mail, broken pencils, notes that have been scribbled – you'll be surprised that this simple two minute task can reduce the unconscious clutter that so easily builds up in our homes.

Dishes

Honesty time – I feel a little bashful about putting in a section on dishes because in my home I don't do any of the dishes! My husband does the hand washing at night and the kids unstack the dishwasher in the morning. But as I've said all along, each family has a different routine, so here are a few tips.

Simple routines make family life run with ease and dealing with dirty (and clean) dishes is one of those areas. Put dishes straight in the dishwasher rather than on the sink, waiting for someone else to put them in. Then when the dishwasher is finished, empty it out straight away so you can start the process over.

If you don't have a dishwasher, fill the sink with soapy water after each meal and whoever is washing can do so quickly.

If there is ever a shortage of concrete in the Australian building industry, my bet is that they'll start using Weet-Bix that have dried in the bowl. Seriously – how can something that my children eat for breakfast with milk have turned to concrete by lunchtime? So for the love of all things good, rinse out bowls before putting them aside to wash. Rant over – that feels better.

Children's Routines

Are those two words even compatible together? *Children's routines.* Your mornings may be more like, 'For the last time, put your shoes on or I'm sending you to school in bare feet!'

Routines aren't about clearing physical clutter; they're about clearing the mental clutter that so easily builds up when you're managing a busy home. Life spins at a rapid pace and sometimes it's hard not to fall off. My hope for you is that a few routines built into your day will free up some headspace for thinking about more important things, or thinking about nothing at all.

Mike Murdock says, 'The secret of your future is hidden in your daily routine.'

Think about times in your day when stress builds up – leaving the house in the morning, after school if you have children, bedtime. These are all times of transition during the day, so putting a routine in place will reduce your stress and enable these times to run a little more smoothly.

For our family, mornings are (usually) straightforward because we have a good routine. The kids know what is expected of them and they remind each other if one forgets … not always nicely, but I'm not claiming a perfect family – just saying our morning routine works! They know that they both need to do their music practice and their chores, and they need to make their school lunch.

This means that of a morning I'm not giving headspace to getting them ready. I'm thinking about whatever client I'm heading out to, preparing myself and attempting to start my day from a place of peace. If your children are preschool age this will not be as straightforward, but once they're in school I found it worked really well.

One routine that I'd highly recommend for any family with kids is that you spend a few minutes before the kids' bedtime doing a quick clean-up of their toys and bedrooms. This teaches children that they need to go to bed with a tidy house, but also means that once they're asleep the night is yours to enjoy.

I find this particularly important for single parent families – the time you get to yourself is so limited that the last thing you want to be doing is cleaning up matchbox cars or trying to find Barbie's missing shoe instead of watching your favourite show or curling up with a good book.

My aim in this chapter is not to make you feel like a 1950s housewife … and for the record, cleanliness is *not* next to godliness – no matter what you've heard! This year for the first time ever I've hired a cleaner and it's so good.

I'm naturally tidy and organised, but mopping and dusting I'll happily leave to someone else. They come once a fortnight and they do an amazing job. My house sparkles once they're finished. I always do my fifteen minute tidy first so they can clean without having to tidy too.

There's no shame or judgement in asking for help. Just because you can do it yourself, doesn't mean you have to. (Same goes for getting in a professional organiser to help you declutter and organise your home.)

I want to help you find efficient ways to run the home if that's your responsibility. And if there's someone else in your family who does these things, let them in on some of the secrets so they experience the freedom too. The more time we free up from household chores, the more time we have for a bush walk, a cuppa with a friend or date night with the hubby.

Remember (write it on the fridge if you need to) that having an organised home is not the end goal – having an organised home is the means to which we free up time for relationships, hobbies, family time and living this awesome life!

Simple Tips

- Think about the chores you do regularly and come up with ways to make them more efficient.
- A tidy house is quicker to clean, so spend fifteen minutes tidying before you try to clean.
- Take the pressure off – routines are good but don't be legalistic. Sickness, holidays, friends in need and sometimes just sitting with a cup of tea and a good book can take priority.

Gifts

'Where am I going to put this?'

William Morris (1834–1896) once said, 'Have nothing in your home that you do not know to be useful, or believe to be beautiful.' He was an English textile designer, poet and novelist. He understood the finer things in life and valued being intentional about what he kept in his home.

What I want to guide you through now is how to deal with an influx of gifts into your home. This is different from when you purchase things yourself. The difference is that with gifts, sometimes they're exactly in line with your style and what you need. And other times, just so *not*.

My mum has a friend who used to buy my sisters and me Christmas presents when we were growing up. She's a beautiful lady – generous, kind and would do anything for you – but gift-giving just wasn't her thing. In my teenage years I remember one particular present I received from her. It was a stick of deodorant. Not a body spray or perfume – literally a roll-on deodorant. I didn't have a problem with body odour; I think she just had no idea what to buy a teenage girl.

I'm going to approach this topic of gifts with sensitivity, but also with diplomacy and honesty. The benefit of dealing with gifts when they enter the home is that you'll avoid filling cupboards with gifts you like, but won't ever use (or just don't like at all!)

Having pre-decided in your mind how you'll handle unwanted gifts will free up the headspace of having to make decisions on the spot or making a new decision each time. A lot of this chapter will have the focus of finding the balance between being a people-pleaser and allowing others to determine how you'll live in and style your home.

Becoming mindful of gift-giving will also enable you to become a more thoughtful gift-giver. You'll come up with new and creative gift ideas that will make people smile and serve your friendships and relationships in ways you'd never imagined.

Let's delve a little deeper into the circumstances around receiving gifts. Here are a few events which might draw such gifts:

- Weddings
- Birthdays
- Christmas
- KK at work
- Housewarming
- Arrival of new baby

I'm yet to come across a client who doesn't have either a cupboard, or space in a cupboard, where they keep unwanted gifts. This doesn't make them ungrateful, rude, picky or snobby. It just means that their taste doesn't always line up with that of the gift-giver. Often the only reason they're still even in the house is because you don't want to offend anyone. And that's a great motive; it's lovely that you want those in your life to feel appreciated.

The question is: can you not keep a gift from someone and still value the friendship? Is it even possible to value the gift but still choose not to keep it?

Gifts are 'things that are given willingly and freely to someone else'. The purpose of a gift can be several things. You might want to show someone that you were thinking of them – to show that you love someone; to show that they are important to you; to encourage someone or make them smile.

For the most part the act of gift-giving is about the relationship between the giver and the receiver. The actual gift is a secondary thing. So next time you get a gift that makes you think, 'Do they even know me?' remember that they thought of you first and then purchased a gift. It's like your mother always said, 'It's the thought that counts.'

I do believe that you can value friendship, value the gift-giver and even value the gift without necessarily bringing the new item out to display in your home. It needs to be done sensitively and compassionately, but it can and needs to be done if you want to keep your home clutter-free.

So … what do you do when someone gives you a gift that is completely unwanted? Well, the answer depends on who the gift is from.

If it's your immediate family and they say, 'If you don't like it you can exchange it,' then maybe take them up on the offer. It might be a little uncomfortable to say that you'd like to exchange it, but I'd suggest that's more respectful of the time and money they've put into it than hiding it away in a cupboard for years. Generally someone won't make that offer if they're not genuine about it – after all, they have tried to find something special for you and that's what they ultimately want for you.

'What if the gift-giver asks if we like it and I can't bear to tell them I hate it?'

I was always taught that if you can't say something nice, don't say anything at all … but I now know that there's always something nice to say. You could honestly say, 'I love that you thought of me,' 'I really like the colour,' or, 'I'm blown away by your generosity.'

All of these statements are true and genuine and can be said without hurting anyone's feelings. It doesn't mean that you then have to keep the gift, though. You have permission to get rid of it.

In our house we have a present box. In here we keep a small number of gifts that we can use for presents. Sometimes I'll see something great on special and buy a few to pop away for gifts. Other times they'll have Lego on sale if you buy three or more, so I buy them and put them away for the next party my kids are invited to.

This is also where we put a gift that's received and either a double or not wanted by the person who received it. For instance, at the moment there is a board game in there that my son received for his birthday from a friend. He already had the board game, so he didn't need a second copy but was happy to put it away and re-gift it when he next goes to a party. No feelings will be hurt, because if the friend comes over and wants to play the game, it's there to play.

Sometimes adult gifts go in there too. I find that the adult gifts in there are good for occasions like work Christmas parties, or Kris Kringle among friends. When the present box is full we put a hold on buying toys on sale until we've used up what's in there (it's not on sale if you don't use it).

The question remains, how exactly do you donate a gift someone has given you that you don't like or won't use? And is there a minimum amount of time you have to keep it first?

Obviously there aren't any hard and fast rules around this, but my suggestion is if you don't like it, you don't keep it.

Don't put it away in the cupboard if you have no intention of using it. Don't even take it out of the box. Donate it to a charity – or if you have a friend who you think would love it, ask them if they'd like to have it.

I don't think there's a minimum time frame you need to keep it for, but maybe leaving it on the bench for a week will help you decide if you really don't like it or if it grows on you. But after that, no more delayed decision-making – remember that delayed decisions around possessions always leads to clutter.

'What if the person who gave me the gift finds out I gave it away?'

I'd simply say to them, 'It was a lovely gift but I found I didn't use it and I didn't want it to go to waste.' Personally (and I don't speak for everyone) I'd much prefer to hear that someone donated a gift I gave them, than find out it's sitting in the back of the cupboard because they don't like it.

'My sister's/mum's/auntie's feelings would be hurt if they found out.'
Note I didn't include brother, dad or uncle in there – because most gifts are purchased by women and most (but not all) men wouldn't be offended at all if they found out you didn't like something they gave you. We have a running joke at Christmas where my dad asks all us kids what he bought us once we've unwrapped our gifts. The card might say 'Love Dad & Mum' but we kids all know who did the shopping.

How do we deal with the pressure of not wanting to hurt anyone's feelings? How can you manage the balance between being a people pleaser and having items displayed around your house that you just don't like, versus being mean and telling people to their face you don't like their gift? Neither of those options are going to serve you well, but somewhere in there – being smiling, grateful and respectful – is middle ground you can learn to feel comfortable in.

So practically, aside from planning for the future, I want you to declutter any gifts you currently have in the cupboard. If you've been married anytime in the last century you're sure to have a few unopened wedding gifts in there. Platters or salad bowls with flowery designs when you prefer white. White coffee mugs when you prefer bright colours. A punch bowl even though you'll never make homemade punch.

The hard things to decide on are gifts that you really like, but for one reason or another you've never found a use for. One such gift for me was a cake stand that we received for our wedding. It's crystal-clear glass and it's beautiful. I love it. I just have never used it in fourteen years of marriage. It's still in the original box and although I wish I had a use for it, the truth is when I bake cakes I serve them on a big round platter that is sturdy and easy to cover if there happens to be cake left at the end of the night.

6. Gifts

I'm sure things are coming to your mind as you read this – thoughtful gifts you've received that you just don't use. So go grab them. Grab every single one of them and donate them to charity. Give yourself permission to let go of gifts you don't use, once and for all.

This isn't a rejection of the people who gave you the gifts – it's you being honest with yourself and saying that you're not going to use them, so they're better off being given to people who will. Storage and space are at such a premium these days that you don't want to use up storage space in your home on things you don't use.

You may also choose to wander around the house at this point to gather any gifts that you've displayed out of obligation, but have never really liked. See it as a clearing out – a decluttering to make way for things you love.

One thing that you'll start to think about as you go through this process is what gifts you've received before and really loved. Gifts that were so *you*, right up your alley and exactly what you would have picked for yourself.

I have a little rule that if I receive soap/moisturiser or candles, I start using them straight away. It's nice to treat yourself and the purpose of these gifts is to be used, not to sit on a shelf and be admired (or sink to the bottom of your bathroom drawer).

> *Delayed decisions around possessions always leads to clutter.*

Final thought when it comes to gifts and decluttering … are there presents you can give that won't become clutter in someone else's home? A few ideas are below; I'm sure you can add many to the list.

- Babysit for a friend's birthday so her husband can take her out to dinner.
- Take a niece or nephew out for an activity instead of buying them toys.
- Take a girlfriend out for a lovely lunch instead of buying her a gift.
- Make a new mum a meal instead of buying her more baby clothes.
- Instead of buying something off a wedding registry you could buy a restaurant voucher for them to celebrate their six month anniversary.
- Offer to help a friend around the house instead of buying a housewarming present – make an afternoon of gardening or painting a room together.

My main take-away for this chapter is that you can love the gift-giver without loving the gift. You can honour the gift-giver without keeping the gift. You can give a gift without giving a physical possession.

Gift-giving is all about showing and receiving love, and sometimes that includes lovely things you'll treasure forever and sometimes it's a gravy boat you'll never use. It's okay to rehome the gravy boat.

6. Gifts

Simple Tips

- Declutter any gifts you've received and don't like or plan to use.

- Create a gift box for items that you'll re-gift if the occasion arises.

- Be mindful when buying gifts for others. Try to give a gift of time if it's a close friend. Your time and friendship are the most valuable gift.

Paperwork

'I can't find my birth certificate anywhere!'

There are plenty of fun things about being an adult. No bed time, chocolate in bed if you so desire, cold pizza for breakfast. You can pick where you live, who you live with, what job you take, how to spend your income. But with freedom comes responsibility – and with responsibility, the inevitable flow of paperwork.

I've yet to meet anyone who is happy having absolutely no order in how papers are kept in their home. Nobody who's happy to have three or four piles of paperwork randomly around the house. Happy to pay late fees; happy to pay interest on credit card bills forgotten about. Nobody aims for that, but most people live exactly like that.

The good news is you don't have to be an accountant or lawyer to successfully manage the flow of papers through your home. Whether you're living on your own, in a share house or managing a family of five, some easy-to-start and simple-to-manage strategies will take the drag out of paperwork.

Something I learnt quickly when I became a professional organiser is that flat surfaces attract clutter. Every single flat surface in your home is like a magnet to paperwork. I'm sure there's a law of physics that's yet to be discovered about the magnetic force flat surfaces have!

Have a quick look around you right now. Whether you're at home, at a café or at work, can you see what I'm talking about? Desks, benches, tables, bedside tables, coffee tables, bookcases … in almost every case there is at least one thing on these surfaces that doesn't belong. And often the culprit is the humble piece of paper.

One major benefit of getting papers organised is that you'll enjoy the benefit of clear flat surfaces again. It's easier to clean, easier to work, and easier to concentrate when you don't have a pile of papers demanding your attention.

A major benefit is how much time you'll save by actioning paperwork when it's received rather than throwing it in a pile to look at later. And then, if you happen to need a document after it has been actioned, you'll know exactly where to find it.

Time is our most precious commodity and as much as I enjoy handling our family's administration, I can think of plenty of things I'd rather do (café, anyone?)

Having your paperwork organised will, of course, save you money. Most late fees cost around $15 and paying unnecessary interest on your credit card can add up to thousands. Surely you've got better things to spend your money on!

7. Paperwork

If you've ever urgently needed a birth certificate or business registration papers you'll know the value of having these things all in one place and easy to grab.

Applying for a passport can be a nightmare if you first need to reapply for a birth certificate. And in the case of a bushfire, if you had time to quickly grab important paperwork it's so much easier to have them all in the same place where you can quickly grab them than rummaging through a filing cabinet, saying to yourself, 'I know it's in here somewhere!'

> *You don't have to be an accountant or lawyer to successfully manage the flow of papers through your home.*

I've identified the biggest reason clients become paper hoarders. It's a new term that I've coined myself and I've got no doubt you'll resonate personally with it. I call it FOTO (Fear of Throwing Out).

The alternative to taking action and organising your papers is that you'll always be searching for the one document you need, wishing that you'd set up a system years ago. The good news is that today is a perfect day to start.

It's actually the best day to start because today is a day when you're not only thinking, 'Gee, I really should get my paperwork under control,' but it's also a day when you're being coached by a professional organiser via an amazing book (if I do say so myself).

Now, no quick promises in this chapter – some areas you can completely declutter and organise in an afternoon. But unless you're still living at home with very minimal outgoing bills, your paperwork and administration will take a little longer. Not weeks – but maybe a few days if you're planning on eating, working and sleeping along the way.

Let's quickly jot down what enters your home under the guise of paperwork, both physical and digital.

- Bills
- Bank statements
- Superannuation statements
- School notices
- School newsletters
- Receipts
- Warranties
- Certificates
- Pharmacy scripts
- Letters/cards
- Invitations
- Advertising
- Contracts
- Legal documents
- Business documentation
- Medical documents

I put 'business documentation' knowing that if you own a business, it'll have its own mountain of paperwork. I won't deal specifically with business paperwork here; if you'd like some customised help in that area, get in touch and I can out to help you individually. Alternatively, your accountant will have some ideas to help with your specific needs.

As you can see, there are lots of different categories for paperwork; it's easy to see how they can all just end up as clutter rather than being organised. My strategy for handling, decluttering and organising paperwork continues my theme of efficiency, not perfection. I'm totally not obsessive about paperwork, but I have a system that works perfectly and is adaptable to any home.

Hot tip number one is to keep all physical papers in one spot. And by that I don't mean in one big pile of paid, unpaid, actioned and yet to be actioned paperwork! I mean have a place in the home that is designated for papers to be actioned, filed and stored. This is likely your admin zone in your home.

I have one client who, when we first started working on her paper flow, confessed that there were papers kept in several parts of the house. Some in the front console as you walk in the door, some on the kitchen bench and others in the study.

Few were ordered, actioned or filed. There were three different piles of unopened mail, bills, school notices, bank statements and credit card bills. It had become overwhelming. So when the piles got too big (or there were guests about to arrive), she'd grab a storage tub and sweep the lot of them into the tub (with the intention of dealing with it 'later').

'Later' never came and piles soon reappeared in these spots, and so the habit of sweeping them into a box but never taking anything out continued.

When she decided enough was enough and got me in to help her create some systems, there were two storage crates filled with papers and a palatable sense of dread that there might be something important in one of those boxes that she'd missed.

Now, let me point out that this client is a professional woman. She works a responsible job and manages a busy household. Her children are delightful, the family is well travelled and their home is beautiful. But because they didn't have a system in place, their paperwork was out of control.

Not all homes I go into are busting at the seams with clutter. Some are after my organisational services to help their homes run more efficiently and to reinstate peace and order in their homes. I enjoy that I work with homes at both ends of the spectrum. (Truth be told, most homes are in need of a good declutter before any productive organisation can happen.)

I tell you this story of my client to encourage you that if you struggle with the paperwork flow in your home, you're not alone. And since the information kept in some paperwork can be sensitive and confidential, you need to know that you can trust the person you're working with. Together we can work out what needs to be actioned, what we need to recycle or shred and how we'll file what's left.

As well as keeping all papers in one spot, my advice is to handle paperwork only once if at all possible.

For example, when a birthday invitation arrives home from school before it goes on the fridge I put the details straight in my diary and immediately reply to the invite. I sometimes feel a bit overeager replying the day we receive the invite, but by replying there and then I only have to handle that invitation the one time and I won't forget about it. How many of you, when sending out invitations for children, sometimes wonder if they'll make it home? Getting that first RSVP is a relief because you know they've reached the correct destination.

Another example is when bills arrive, either by mail or email. I handle bills the day they arrive and schedule them to be paid the day they are due (I do this online).

Once they are set to be paid, I throw them straight away. Only having to handle them once is such a time saver. No rushing to pay something before it's due, never having to pay late fees and no pile sitting on my desk begging for my attention.

If getting rid of all bills scares you, you could keep just the most recent bill and replace it whenever a newer version arrives.

Same goes for school notices if you have kids. The day they come home or the email arrives is the day they get filled out and they're always returned the following day. It's too easy for them to become lost otherwise.

Another quick tip is to read the school/kinder newsletter the day it arrives with your phone or planner in hand. Then you can enter important dates straight into your calendar and the newsletter can be deleted or thrown out when you're done.

I recommend getting as much work paperwork digitally as possible. What we need to physically keep is decreasing each year.

Once you've pooled all your paperwork in one spot (have a basket or tray so everyone in the family knows where it goes) and you've handled bills and notices straight away, the question remains – 'What do I do with the rest and how do I file what I need?'

The first mistake that people make is they go out and buy a filing cabinet. Don't do that! And if you already have a filing cabinet I'm going to show you how you can get rid of it and reclaim space in your home.

Instead of using a cumbersome filing cabinet, inboxes, filing boxes, coloured folders, tabs and whatever else you've purchased over the years, I'm going to tell you blow by blow how I handle paperwork (this is specifically for the home, but my businesses are done with the same method – just adjusted to the business needs).

Hopefully it goes without saying that you can just modify this to suit your family needs. You may have more or less paperwork than I do, but this will give you an idea.

First, here is a list of what I use

- A basket/box/tray for all incoming papers to be put in (at least A4 size)
- 1x storage box with a lid (A4 size)
- 1x ring binder folder
- Pack of 50 clear plastic pockets
- 5x document wallets

First thing is to place the basket/tray/box for all incoming papers where all family members can reach and see. For us this is on my desk, but clients have it in the kitchen, on a workstation or at the front door.

Everyone needs to get used to putting things in there. Mail, advertising, notices and bills – literally anything that comes through the door that's paperwork.

In our family I do all the administration because frankly I love it. Call me strange, but I enjoy paying the bills, balancing the budget and filling in forms (aside perhaps from Centrelink ones!) But in your family it might be a combination of people who need to access the paperwork, so make it clear where it will be kept at all times.

Next thing to grab is the storage box with a lid. This is where you'll keep all warranties and manuals. Not filed, not in date order – just all in together in a box. Because for the number of times you actually need to claim a warranty or refer to a manual, you can quickly go through the box and find what you're looking for. Most manuals are online so if you're not fussed about keeping manuals, skip this step.

If we needed to 'file' them in some special order then it's just another job to put off. By having permission to just throw them in a box, they'll actually end up in there and you can find what you need when you need it. Remember – efficiency, not perfection.

Next, we're going to set up the 'current' ring binder folder. Put about thirty plastic pockets in there because this will become your filing cabinet for the year. If you have paperwork to keep, this is where they'll go. So one plastic pocket for pharmacy scripts, one for receipts, one for utilities, one for tax deductible donations, and so on.

You get the idea – as things arrive that you need to keep you set them up in their own pocket. The beauty of this system is that at the end of each financial year, you have all the important documents you need to do your tax return in one portable place.

Once your tax return is complete each year, grab your current year folder and throw out anything you don't need to keep for taxation purposes (please check with your accountant for personalised advice).

Gas and electricity bills, phone bills, rates, water bills – things that if you needed them in the future, you could just call the provider and ask for a copy – can be recycled. With what's left, pop it all in one of your document wallets and label the financial year.

I keep things like our tax return, receipts for things we've claimed and other items like insurance papers. Then the plastic pockets all get put together and kept with the prior four-years folders.

Each year has its own document wallet and I can grab them quickly if I need something. Most people only need to keep at most five years of receipts/documents, so I just keep reusing the same folders. The folders are handy because if you pick a folder up the wrong way you'll avoid spilling a year's worth of receipts on the floor.

If you're currently working with a full filing cabinet it might be quite a job to reduce it to a folder for each year and a box of warranties and manuals, but the effort will be worth it.

The last category of paperwork that we need to manage is our important documents. Honestly, there aren't a stack of these in our lives – just a few, but it's so important to keep these together, safe and accessible.

My suggestion is to keep these documents at the back of the 'current year' ring binder folder. Because this folder is always for the current year it's always the one you're using on a daily or weekly basis.

7. Paperwork

Keep your important documents in plastic pockets where you can clearly see what's there. We keep our birth certificates, marriage certificate, copies of our licence and the kids' immunisation certificates in there.

These are now easy to find when you're trying to apply for family assistance or applying for a new passport. You may also keep things like a copy of your resume and an itinerary if you've got travels planned. These stay in the folder permanently.

Should I ever have the scary situation of having to evacuate my house in an emergency, if I have time I know exactly which folder to grab.

So … time for a few queries you might have.

'We run a business from home so we need to keep a filing cabinet for all the paperwork.'

Maybe you do, but maybe there is a more efficient way of keeping your paperwork. Clearly labelled folders could work just as well and make things easier to find.

Maybe look into whether your accounting software keeps electronic copies of invoices and receipts? You may not have to keep as much as you think.

Filing cabinets tend to rarely be decluttered so you may find catalogues and brochures from suppliers that are years out of date. Think outside the box, but if a filing cabinet is going to work best for you, then go for it. Just keep it to business paper so business and personal are separate.

'What if I need it but I threw it out?'

I usually hear this question from baby boomers. This is because they learnt about paperwork and filing before the digital age and it's a fair question. How difficult is it to get a copy of a bill? How easy is it to get a bank statement from three years ago?

If you're concerned about throwing out a type of bill, a quick call to the provider will let you know if you can access archived bills. I'm certainly not advocating a completely paper-free home (maybe one day!) but I want you to ask the questions, 'Do I really need this?' and, 'Could I get a copy quickly if I needed to?'

Reducing paper clutter in your home will free your time, avoid unnecessary costs and make finding what you need much simpler. I've never met anyone who had a simple and working system for handling paperwork that would give it up. You can be that person – you can do it and you can succeed at it. Give it a go!

Xrays

A funny thing that I've come across in a few homes is a collection of x-rays. I think back in the day patients were required to keep these and bring them to future appointments. But now, x-rays and their reports are kept electronically and shared with doctors and specialists that need to review them.

If you've got old x-rays sitting around, don't throw them in the bin. X-rays need to be recycled because they contain a small amount of hazardous waste and also contain a small amount of silver, which can be recovered through the recycling process. Your local council or doctor's clinic will be able to advise where to dispose of them, or you can visit www.recyclingnearyou.com.au/xray.

Simple Tips

- Create a place where all incoming paperwork goes.
- Build a simple filing system (current, forever and five year archive).
- Have a box for all manuals and warranties.

Kids Artwork

*I*f you're a Pinterest mum I'm sure you've seen the many wonderful ways you can display your children's artwork that they bring home. You can create hanging displays, frame them, make them into birthday cards and a thousand other creative projects.

I'm not going to suggest you take digital photos of every piece that comes into the house and then print out yearly hardcover books to showcase their artistic talent. If that's the stuff you love doing with your child then I cheer you on! Remember, I'm not advocating perfection so my solution is way more functional.

Here's how it works in my house. A piece of artwork comes into the house. I *ooh* and *ah* and point out the things I like about the piece.

If it's a standout piece we have a few Ikea frames in the hallway for kids' art and we can put it in one of those (taking out what's already in there). But generally the pieces get enjoyed for an afternoon and then the kids (not my husband or me) decide what to do with it.

They have two options. They can either put it in their special box or put it in the recycling. The recycling is self-explanatory (my boys put it in a box next to the fire to burn – but perhaps not the most sensitive approach if your child would find that upsetting).

Their special box is a storage container that lives under each child's bed. This box is their domain. The only rule is that the lid must always go back on. This means that when they bring home a pile of school work that they want to keep, if it's already full they need to curate what they keep and what goes.

Art and drawings from home go in there too; this is the entirety of their collection of work. I think it's reasonable to contain that to one box.

Something that I love to see is that a couple of times a year I'll find one of my children sitting in their bedroom with all their work set out around them. They're looking back at work they did at kinder, maybe their first drawing – they love a walk down memory lane. It's a solution that works really well for our family; it's inexpensive and versatile enough to fit almost any family situation.

Garage and Junk Room

'What if I need it?'

Do you have a shed? A garage or carport? Do you have a spare room? Do you have storage under the house or in the roof? If you answered yes to any of these questions then this chapter is for you. If you've ever muttered the words, 'What if I need it?' then gather in, because we need to talk.

Between 1984 and 2011, the size of the average Australian home doubled in size. Double! I grew up in a family of six (later to become seven) and we had three bedrooms, one bathroom and one lounge room. This was normal.

Yet now it's not uncommon to have spare bedrooms, media rooms, rumpus rooms, double or triple garages and storage that my mum could only have dreamed of when we were growing up.

Despite all the extra space and on average fewer people living in that space, I still hear, 'We just don't have enough storage,' fairly regularly. If those words have come from your mouth (and they've come from mine) then hold on to your spare bike because we're delving into the world of 'Use It or Lose It'.

Imagine in your mind's eye what driving into a clutter-free garage would feel like. What it would feel like to open the shed on a Saturday morning to grab the whipper snipper without having to climb over a wheelbarrow and chainsaw first. Imagine all the 'stuff' that lines the walls of the garage and try to tally up in your head how much money you've spent. Actually, maybe stop there – that might be getting a little too close for comfort!

Sometimes we go about our daily lives totally unaware of the clutter we've collected around us. It's not until we get back from a holiday, or have someone important coming to visit, or we decide to list the house on the market that we realise how much stuff there is.

Wouldn't it feel great to clear out under the stairs or have a hallway cupboard that has empty shelves? Wouldn't it feel more relaxed to know you only keep in the garden shed what you actually use month by month? You would feel less guilt about how much stuff you had if you actually knew what you owned – and owned only what you used. Having a minimal carbon footprint is important to many of us, and this means we need to be mindful consumers.

Home insurance agencies estimate that the average home has a huge $173,000 worth of contents inside.[2] How much of that have you purchased but not used? How much is sitting around depreciating while you work hard to pay it off?

---

2. 'How Much Are The Average Aussie's Contents Worth?', Compare The Market, <https://www.comparethemarket.com.au/blog/home-contents/average-aussies-contents-worth/>

8. Garage and Junk Room

I'm constantly amazed how many people have expensive cars sitting in their driveways because their garages are too full of stuff to fit the car inside. Your car is one of your most expensive possessions; why leave it out in the weather when you have a garage purpose-built for it? Unless you make a determined decision to make a change, nothing will shift and your garage/shed/spare room will continue to be cluttered by items you once purchased but no longer use.

To get your brain ticking over on what these items might be for you, here are a few examples of things my clients have been keeping but not using.

- Patio heaters
- Kids' garden toys (ride-on bikes, swings, slides)
- Garden tools
- Exercise equipment
- Bikes
- Furniture
- Sports equipment
- Adult children's childhood possessions
- Outdoor furniture
- Camping equipment
- Vehicles (cars, motorbikes, jet skis and boats)
- Broken items to be fixed

The list could go on and on because every family is different and we all keep different things. I'm yet to find a home where I couldn't turn up with a two metre cube skip and fill it with unused items in half a day.

So how do we go about reclaiming our space and storing what we need to in smart ways? Let's start outside. Do you have a broken swing set, busted trampoline or old cubby that hasn't been used for years? You become so used to these items being in your backyard you didn't even notice they're there until I brought them to your attention. Do you have 'outside toys' that have long been forgotten? Are there bikes that have been grown out of or scooters that are too small? These things all contribute to the feeling of clutter in your home.

There are items stored away in garages that you don't want to throw out – they might be worth money or still have good use left in them. For these items I'd suggest trying to sell them online.

If you purchased a water pressure cleaner but never use it, it's time to go. If you purchased a treadmill but it's now gathering dust in the spare room, it's time to go. If you purchased a new couch and the old one is sitting in the garage, it's time to go.

Here are a couple of questions you could ask yourself as you come across unused items:

- If it broke, would I replace it?
- If I saw it in the shop today, would I buy it?
- Have I had good value from this item?
- Is this item worth the space it takes up?

As well as taking up both physical and mental space, these unused items are also locking up your hard earned money. If you purchased a blower for the garden or a drop saw for the shed, have you used these items enough to justify the hundreds of dollars you now don't have? You don't pay for possessions with money; you pay with hours of your life. How long did it take you to earn the $500 to buy that thing you just had to have? It's confronting for sure, but it's a question to ponder next time you want to buy something you're not sure if you'll use.

Think about some alternatives to buying when you need something for a particular job. Is it something you can hire? Is there a neighbour or family member you can borrow it from? Could you do a trade swap with someone where they could do the job for you and you could offer them a service in return? Sometimes it would even be cheaper to hire a professional rather than buy the equipment to do it yourself.

> *You don't pay for possessions with money; you pay with hours of your life.*

Now, how to organise that which is left and is either used regularly or is a seasonal item.

I'm a *huge* fan of large plastic storage tubs for storing big items or collections of items, especially when they are being stored in garages or sheds. If you have a whole collection of gardening hand tools, for example, keep them together in a tub so you can always find what you need.

The principle here is exactly the same as inside the house. Keep like items together and if everything has a home it's easier to find what you're looking for and then pack up. The beauty of these containers is that they stack easily, seal closed and even if the garage is dusty, what's inside will stay clean and dry.

Sports Equipment

For seasonal sporting items like cricket sets, grab a large tub and put inside the pads, bats, wickets, balls and anything else needed for cricket season.

Have a container for water activity toys (floaties, balls, body boards, water guns) and you can chuck this in the car when you're visiting the beach without having to search around for each thing individually.

Bikes

If you have a whole collection of bikes that lean on each other and are difficult to get to when you need them, have a look at alternative storage options. Having to work a pedal of one bike out of the spokes of another is enough to put me off riding all together, so having them easy to access is key.

Friends of mine have hung all their bikes from the ceiling of their garage; they're out of the way and take up no room on the floor.

We don't have a garage, so we purchased a bike parking rack online (like you see outside public buildings) that you wheel the front wheel into and the bike stands on its own. We have our bikes locked up to this and it's so easy to access the bikes when we need them. They don't touch each other so it's easy to grab a bike from the middle if we need to.

In terms of helmets, locks, bike pumps, etc. – again, grab a plastic tub and keep it all in together. Much better than picking up your helmet from the garage floor and finding a white tail spider inside!

Camping

I love camping, and we don't do enough of it. We have all the gear – a huge tent, big gazebo, camping pantry, stove, camp chairs, mattresses, foam mats, camping cooking equipment, folding table and benches, and a big storage tub of camping crockery, utensils, cups, etc. Now that's a *lot* of stuff to store for something we only do a few times a year, but to us, it's worth it.

If you're a family that camps then here are a few tips that help our family pack and prepare for a camping trip without too much hassle.

Firstly, no surprises – we use plastic storage containers. One has all our kitchenware in it, everything from frying pans to cutlery and utensils. Another has our blow up mattresses.

Our tent, gazebo and all our other 'large' items are stacked together in our shed. Everything is together in one place and although I wish we had a garage to keep them in instead of a shed, we make do with what we have.

The only things that are for camping and don't live in the shed are our folding chairs and sleeping bags. Purely and simply, this is because I'm scared of spiders and would never use one again if they were stored in the shed!

If you can keep everything together for an activity like camping, when it comes to packing the car you can just pick up all the equipment from the one place and when you're done it gets put away easily as well.

Christmas

Let me park here for a minute to talk about Christmas and how to best store everything you need for this fun season of the year. When we talk about seasonal items that you want to keep, but need to store away, Christmas decorations is the first thing that comes to mind. Whether you're an average Christmas decorator or if you go all out and light up the street, the same principles will apply.

Firstly, it's important to keep all electrical items in sealed, durable containers and kept dry. So please don't pack your Christmas lights into the cardboard box they came in and then leave them in the attic all year. House fires over the Christmas season can all too often be traced back to faulty Christmas lights.

So grab a container and keep all your Christmas things in there. Keep decorations, ornaments, tinsel, lights, garden decorations and whatever else you have for decorating in there also. This makes decorating at Christmas so much easier when you only need to grab one or two (or a few more if you're really into it) containers. It's also much easier to pack up when everything can go in together.

Something I teach my clients is to keep everything Christmas together. This includes special tablecloths you might use, or special crockery and glasses that traditionally have been kept in a kitchen cupboard for the 364 days they're not in use.

If you're a super organised person and buy bonbons for the following year in the Christmas sales, then keep these in here too. Christmas cards that you purchased on sale – in they go. My kids have a special Christmas puzzle and a few special Christmas teddies – these are also in our Christmas boxes, because the magic of them is that they only come out at Christmas time. You might do the same with books, nativity scene toys, etc.

You can see how practical this is when at the start of December you decide to set up a tree and start getting ready for Christmas. Everything you need is together and not taking up precious space around the home at other times of the year.

Can I encourage you that if you take advantage of the post-Christmas sales and buy new Christmas decorations, you get rid of broken or shabby ones that you're unlikely to use the following year. Tinsel rarely lasts more than a year or two and some homemade decorations barely last the year they're made, so don't hold onto things you know you won't use again.

Christmas cards (and birthday cards) certainly aren't as popular as they used to be, but we still have a few that come in. Some people will keep every card they're ever given (more people than you'd imagine, actually!) If you have one incredibly special card then give yourself permission to keep it, but for all other cards, leave them out til Christmas to enjoy and then at the end of that time, gather them all together, re-read them and then throw them out. Christmas cards aren't meant to be kept for years. Enjoy them over the Christmas period and then let them go.

Home Projects

What about projects that are half done or broken things you're intending to fix that are in the garage or shed? Do you keep them for when you've got time, or do you let them go because if you haven't done it so far it's unlikely you'll get to it?

My general advice is that if the project has been sitting for more than a year, it's not a priority – so time to throw it out. Your time is your most valuable asset, and unless you love a good handy project, take the pressure off and get rid of the broken thing you intended to fix. If you've lived without it for a year while it waited to be fixed, you won't miss it.

Don't collect free furniture that you could 'do up' unless you know how to restore furniture. Don't take old wardrobes to a new house if the new house already has built-ins. You'll end up storing it in the garage and filling it with clutter. Think carefully about keeping something you don't know how you'll use when you upgrade. Old TVs, couches, bedframes and bookshelves rarely get used again and you'll end up throwing it out one day, so why not clear it out now and have the space to breathe?

And when you're done, please park your car inside the garage where it belongs. Then ring your insurance agency and ask for a discount because your car is locked up inside at night!

Simple Tips

- Ask yourself, 'If this broke would I replace it?' If not, it can probably go.
- Keep like items together and store in clear plastic containers.
- Make some money by selling items you don't use; have a garage sale or sell online.

Sentimental Items

'But it reminds me of my nanna!'

*H*eirlooms hold special memories, bonds and connections to loved ones. How do we treat them with the respect they deserve and enjoy the memories they bring for generations to come? What do we do when a family member passes away or heirlooms are passed down from our parents to us?

There are two different types of heirlooms: 'I really should keep this,' and, 'I really want to keep this.'

Both are quite emotive statements that deserve us digging deeper. The what, why, who, how and when all require thought as we sort through the heirlooms in our homes. Whether you've been given the heirlooms directly or they've been passed down through generations, these questions will apply.

Giving headspace to items passed down through the family will help honour your memories. My hope is that you'll enjoy the journey and feel at peace about decisions you make along the way. This may be part of the grieving process for you, regardless of how long ago the person passed away. It should also remind you of the values, stories and life of the person or people you want to remember.

Heirlooms are things passed down from elderly family or family members who have passed away. They usually enter our lives after loss and carry with them strong emotions. The emotions can be right across the spectrum – from joy and peace to guilt, shame and despair.

Heirlooms can attach themselves to the emotions you were feeling when you received the item. If your pa gave you his war medals while he was still alive you might remember them with pride. But if you received a teapot after his death you may feel grief and loss every time you see it. It's almost like just by seeing the item you return in an instant to the feelings you were experiencing when you received them.

I've had many clients start to cry even by looking at the box that contains their heirlooms. With tears streaming down their cheeks, I have the privilege of hearing their stories. Stories of bravery, courage and loss. Stories that often don't relate at all to the actual items passed down, but speak volumes of the legacy left to family still here.

I love asking questions about stories and memories passed down. I like seeing your eyes light up as you talk of your nanna's passion for her garden or your auntie's almond cake you loved as a child. I love seeing the photo of your mum holding you at birth and of you and your sister up a tree at your dad's farm. Losing family is so tough – and while some memories will fade, there is power in storytelling. There is a legacy built and memories stirred.

Amidst the storytelling and reminiscing, there must also be truth.

9. Sentimental Items

If you're the kind of person who seems to attract all kinds of heirlooms from relatives you weren't even close to, you need to know this: you're not the eternal guardian for your family's possessions. Saying no to a grieving family member is hard to do, so instead of feeling like you have to make decisions in a time of grief, ask for time. Ask for a month before making any decisions about what you'd like to keep or before you have to say yes to bringing something into your home.

In some situations time can be a limiting factor if you need to prepare a home for sale or vacate a unit. Go with your gut in this case – make the decision you feel most comfortable with at the time and only take an item that you would use or display.

Let's explore the 'why' of heirlooms. Originally heirlooms were expensive jewellery or precious antiques that were passed from one generation to the next because of their value. It was your inheritance. You didn't receive money in a will like people sometimes do now – the value was in the possessions that the person owned and passed on. As time has passed it has become not about valuable antiques, but rather a way to remember someone special.

So with this being the case, the why of heirlooms and inheritance has changed significantly over time. It used to be to help set you up in life – now it's about memory.

So this also impacts on the kind of things people have as keepsakes to a passed family member. Whereas it used to be jewellery and antiques, most of what I see now includes crockery sets, cutlery, ornaments and personal possessions (like walking sticks, war medals and sewing kits). The reason most heirlooms are kept and passed along is not because they're worth a lot of money should someone want to cash it in someday – but rather because they remind you of the times you shared. So with this in mind, how can you give due honour to the things you wish to keep?

I'm often at someone's home when they pull out a box of fabric, dolls, crockery, clothes, etc. and tell me that it was given to them after their nanna passed away. The box always seems to be hidden away at the top of a cupboard, gathering dust.

Firstly, I'd say to get them out of the back of the cupboard. If they're important to you they don't belong hidden away. Get them all out and lay them on a bed or on the kitchen table. If you've got heirlooms from multiple people, then gather together all the things from your nanna in one area, from your dad in the other and so on. See how many things you have – you may never have had it all out together before, so it may surprise you how much you've kept.

Pick one pile to go through first (I'd suggest the easiest pile). Are there things in there that don't really remind you of that person? They may have been owned by them, but the memories you have with them aren't around that item? For these things, offer them to other family members if they'd like it; if no one puts their hand up you can donate it.

It's important to not pass judgement on how other family members treat inherited items. Each family member processes grief and loss in a different way. My grandmother recently was moved into a nursing home and each grandchild was invited into her home to pick something they'd like to keep that reminded them of her. My memories with my grandma are captured in some lovely photos and letters that she's written me over the years, but nothing physically in her home triggered those memories for me. My younger sister, however, felt a deep connection to some beautiful furniture pieces and now proudly displays them in her home. Two sisters, same family, but heirlooms mean different things to us.

If you're already in possession of heirlooms you no longer want to keep, you can offer them to family: 'These have been in my cupboard for years and they're just not my style. My memories of [Aunt Kate] aren't dependant on these items, would anyone else like them?' Don't be upset if nobody decides to take it. Just let them know that you'll be donating it and then you're free to do so.

Do you have full sets of something (like crockery) where you'd never use a full set, but you could keep just one? A client had this with a set of crockery passed down to her husband from his great aunt. It was African themed with giraffes in the centre of each plate, but it didn't fit their personal style. So rather than keep the whole set in the kitchen cupboard, which was where it had current residency, we kept one plate, one bowl and one side plate and donated the rest to charity. Now it's a nice set on display whenever they open the cupboard.

Another client had inherited boxes and boxes of fabric from her grandmother who, like her, was a seamstress. Some of the material was lovely, but some was aged and discoloured. So she tenderly (and with tears) went through the boxes to keep what she loved or thought she could use in the future. What she had left was a small collection of beautiful fabrics that we stored in sealed containers to avoid any further deterioration.

I've seen clients who have been passed down a wedding dress, ball gown or military uniform, take a small portion of the fabric and frame it alongside a photo of their relative. This is such an appropriate way to honour memory – much more powerful than having these things hidden away.

There are some really great sized shadow boxes you can purchase which are perfect for displaying heirlooms. We have one on our wall that contains a single foot booty that my grandma knitted for my son when he was born. I wanted to keep the booties, but having them in the bottom of a drawer hardly seemed fitting. So I kept only one and framed it alongside our family photos. It looks so perfect up there.

If you've got antique cutlery, these would fit perfectly in a shadow box that could be displayed in your kitchen. Take one of each item (knife, fork, spoon, etc.) and frame them together on a lovely piece of paper. Then you capture the memory without having to keep a box of cutlery you'll never use. Medals, jewellery and watches can also be framed like this and would look stunning on the wall in a walk-in robe or bathroom. Think creatively about how you could display the things that matter most to you and you'll smile each time you walk past and remember a person dear to you.

If you've got children, another area that's very similar to heirlooms is their baby memories. These are gifts or mementos from special occasions in their lives. Do you still have the pregnancy test from when you first found out you were pregnant? Do you have the hospital tags your newborn wore home? Do you have their first outfit kept away somewhere?

I recently was working with a client who had kept so much of her only child's baby clothes that there was a wardrobe full in the house. She'd kept a christening gown, first outfit, school uniforms and many other special outfits. (Her child was now in her twenties and didn't want the items herself). I hear the disappointment from clients almost weekly who have saved things for when their children grow up and the now-adult children don't want them. The item is special to the mum, but doesn't hold any meaning for their child. Parents keep their children's primary school uniform because it brings back memories of their young family, but are hurt when their grown children don't want to keep it.

In these situations I think healthy honesty is always best. Always acknowledge the thought behind the action. 'Wow Mum, that's amazing that you kept it for so long. I'm sure I've got a photo of me in that outfit. I appreciate the offer, but I don't want to keep it – having the photo is enough for me.' Don't ever mock someone for keeping things, no matter how silly you feel it is. They are kept because they're important to someone you love. Appreciate that someone loves you this much and show respect while speaking the truth in love.

Something that is particularly hard is when you don't want to keep an inherited item any longer, but you feel you'll hurt someone's feelings if you give it away. How do you have that conversation? Do you even have the conversation or do you just get rid of it? What about when one person in a relationship wants to keep something and the other person desperately wants to get rid of it?

I suggest grace, love, understanding and time. Remember we talked about how heirlooms can have really strong feelings attached to them? Well, when you think someone is being irrational or unreasonable, stop and remember to try to understand. Help them process. Ask what memories they have of the person and how they'd like to honour that person in their life. The issue is very rarely about the actual item, but rather the feelings attached.

In the rare case that you've inherited antiques that are worth money, should you keep them out of obligation or is it okay to sell them? Firstly, I'd say that before you try to sell them, I'd check if any other family members want to keep the item first. And if not, go ahead and sell the item/s. You may choose to use the money to do something in memory of your loved one. Maybe a go on a holiday or book an experience that you'll always remember.

We received an inheritance a few years ago and we used the money to buy a piano, because the family member who gave us the money always used to love listening to me play the piano as a child. Now my children are learning the piano and it's special to me that they have the same opportunity I had growing up.

Are you keeping any heirlooms to give to your children? It's okay if you are – I have just a few tips for you. Firstly, keep them in a safe place – a sealed container is best so they don't get ruined or broken.

Secondly, keep items that are manageable or small. A hand painted vase is going to be easier to pass down than a suitcase of fine china.

Also, you may wish to wait until your child is an adult and can fully appreciate the gift they're being given. I know that even in my twenties I wouldn't have seen the value in a family item passed down, so don't rush the process.

Finally, offer the item to your child rather than thrusting it upon them and guilt them into keeping it. Guilt is a terrible motivator – it just breeds resentment and heirlooms are meant to bring joy and memories, definitely not make you feel guilt.

One of the most amazing things I've found when working with a client was her dad's ashes. We were going through a wardrobe, pulling out everything that had been stored on the top shelf. We pulled out torches, camping gear, fairy lights and then right at the back she discovered the urn containing her dad's ashes. It was quite an amazing experience – she felt joy to have found them and a simmer of guilt that the family hadn't yet spread his ashes.

It was such an encouragement to hear that not long after we found them, she'd gathered her siblings together and they'd laid his ashes. I get all emotional just thinking about how decluttering led to this beautiful moment for a very special family. Being a professional organiser, I get to participate in some really raw, vulnerable moments with clients and it's always an honour to be walking through these moments together.

9. Sentimental Items

> *Heirlooms are meant to bring joy and evoke memories.*

I retell this story to clients when they have an 'oh, I forgot I even owned this' moment or they discover a special thing a passed parent gave to them. It's so rewarding to see clients discover something they love or have been looking for.

Simple Tips

- For heirlooms you wish to keep, decide how you can display or use them.

- Unwanted inherited items can be sold, donated or offered to family members.

- Become an encourager – tell family members how much they mean to you while you have the chance. Rather than gifts, prioritise sharing memories. A cup of tea or doing a puzzle together is time well spent and memories are made in that moment.

Organised Medications

An area of people's homes that can be totally forgotten about when decluttering is medicines. People will put them all together in a box like I suggest, but forget that medications have expiry dates and so need to be inspected individually.

Medications are also expensive, so before you head off to the chemist to pick up a cream for bites or cough medicine, check first what you have already. Rather than always buying a new bottle and throwing out the half you didn't use, take advantage of what you already have if it's suitable.

Of course, never *ever* share prescription medication with anyone, even if you have the same illness. Dose recommendations will often change depending on who it's for and your doctor will know if a new medication will interact with any other medicine you're on.

A few tips regarding decluttering and organising your medicines:

- When you buy vitamins for a reason (naturopath or doctor's recommendation), keep using them for the recommended time. If you're told magnesium will help your muscle cramps, don't just take supplements for two weeks and then stop. You've already paid for the whole bottle, so continue with your recommended dose for the recommended time.
- Keep all medications out of the reach of children; even if your kids are older you still need to monitor what's being administered.
- If your child is taking several medications for a sickness (like Panadol and antibiotics), it can help to write on a piece of paper on the fridge the exact time each medication is taken. Then when you visit the doctor or a hospital, you can just take it with you so you remember what they've had.
- If you have a prescription cream but can't remember what it was for, throw it away.
- If you have five bottles of sunscreen, don't buy any more until you've used up what you already have.
- Keep your scripts in your 'current folder' so that when you need to fill a repeat script, you know where to find it and don't have to make another doctor appointment to get it reissued.
- If you have to take daily medication but sometimes forget, speak to your pharmacist about ways to build it into your schedule. Consider buying a pill box that has compartments for each day of the week. Just make sure you also keep this out of the reach of children.
- Disposal of medication is important. If you're not sure how to get rid of a particular medicine, return it to your local pharmacy and they'll dispose of it for you.

Storage

'I'll just use a storage unit ...'

I'm a self-confessed Ikea fanatic. I love the small house displays they set up in-store and I secretly dream of being able to live in such a compact space. When the catalogue/magazine arrives in the mail each year it's better than Christmas – I get a pot of peppermint tea (and a block of Cadbury Rocky Road) and I set aside a whole afternoon just to sit, read and dream about beautiful functional storage.

I can spend hours wandering through their stores, planning solutions for our house or coming up with creative ideas for clients. It's like my happy place. Sometimes I go as a consultant for friends or family – they'll show me a problem area in their home before we go to Ikea together with measurements and I help them pick the perfect furniture for their space. I also regularly get to go to Ikea with or for clients.

When I shop on my own for something in particular, I can be in and out in fifteen minutes because I know every little shortcut and where every item is kept. I'm almost at the point where I know the names of so many of the products, I'd classify as bilingual.

My husband, on the other hand, hates being dragged around Ikea. He's scared we'll get lost or we'll buy something we can't put together.

I'm the ultimate Ikea assembly woman. As part of my shopping service, some clients also hire me to assemble their storage units for them; they claim if they try to do it on their own they'll end up throwing it, breaking it or fighting with their partner. When it comes to sturdy, durable, functional, affordable and environmentally conscience storage they are the best (in my humble opinion).

You can tell – I love Ikea! But there's a balance, because even too much storage can become clutter. If storage isn't purposeful, functional and utilised then it's not adding value to you or your home.

Something I pride myself on is helping clients make the most of the storage they already have in their homes, because using what you have well enables you to see and access the items that you're storing inside.

I love multifunctional storage, like a TV unit with drawers underneath for gaming console storage or a mudroom entrance that can store umbrellas, spare change and shopping bags. I especially love a multifunctional laundry; of all the rooms in the house that you can make functional and beautiful, it's the humble laundry!

Another great thing about storage is that by storing items correctly, you can keep them in good condition and it's easy to find what you're looking for when you need something quickly.

10. Storage

A favourite and well repeated saying of mine is, 'A home for everything and everything in its home.' I don't have anything in my house that doesn't have a home. It's a big statement, but it's true. Every single item in our home has a place where it belongs.

When anything new comes in we consciously decide where it's going to live. It's not a cumbersome exercise because there are zones and natural places that things go. This habit has served us brilliantly over the years because nothing gets lost in our home and we never waste time looking for something.

Right now without getting out of your seat, can you name for me where the following items are?

- Your phone charger
- Your tax return from last year
- Your slippers
- Your birth ceftificate
- Your sunglasses
- A box of tissues
- AA batteries
- A flat head screwdriver
- Your bathers
- Your umbrella

How did you go? Did you get all ten? Maybe four or five – or only one? Were you able to name where they are but not where they belong?

Being intentional about where you keep your possessions is key to having an organised home and key to keeping a decluttered home. Finding things becomes easier, packing things away becomes simple and even packing for holidays becomes streamlined when there is a home for everything and everything is in its home.

I met someone the other day and as we got talking I mentioned that I was a professional organiser. She started telling me that her garage had been so full with clutter that she couldn't park the car in there, and could hardly squeeze in there herself when she needed to find something. She said it was so chockers that she just had to do something about it.

I expected her to say she'd booked a skip or that she'd like to book me in to help, but instead she went on to tell me that she'd gone to the shops and purchased a hundred large plastic tubs and was filling them up and storing them back in the garage.

She was so proud of herself for 'getting organised' but sadly had missed the cause of the problem. Her problem was not a lack of plastic storage tubs. Clutter is clutter, whether it's in plastic containers or not. If you don't need it, don't want it or don't use it, then fair to say it's unnecessary and cluttering up your home.

Francine Jay says, 'Your home is living space, not storage space.' Sadly, as the size of our homes has doubled so has the amount of possessions we store in them. Instead of living more, we're just storing more.

Choosing not to do anything about clutter will result in one of two things: you'll either continue to live in clutter, losing things and doubling up on things you already own; or you'll keep purchasing containers and hiding the real problem.

Or worse still – and I know some of you are already in this boat – you'll take out a self-storage unit and start paying someone else to keep your abundance of possessions.

10. Storage

Let's park for a minute on the topic of self-storage units. Australia currently has a $1 billion dollar self-storage market![3] That's a lot of money spent on storing items people don't use.

You've heard the saying, 'out of sight, out of mind' – well, that's exactly what the self-storage industry relies on. They rely on you not being able to make decisions about possessions that you own – and then once you put them in storage you forget about it and leave it there.

I've never met someone who intended on using their storage unit for years; it's always taken out with the intention of using it for 'six months maximum'. Storage units cost their renters a minimum of $2000 per year. Add that up over a few years and the rent has probably cost you more than the value of what you're storing. Sorry (although not too sorry) if this is hitting a nerve for you because you're paying a bill each month to a self-storage company.

The companies themselves aren't evil or out to scam people; the truth is they're responding to a need in the market. We've driven that need as a culture and society and if we want to change our personal relationship with 'stuff', then we can.

> ***If storage isn't purposeful, functional and utilised then it's not adding value to you or your home.***

---

3. 'Self-Storage Services in Australia: Market Research Report', IbisWorld, <http://www.ibisworld.com.au/industry-trends/specialised/market-research/consumer-goods-services/self-storage-services.html>

So what do you do if you already rent a storage unit and are now reconsidering the investment? Work out how much it costs you each year in fees. Then, my suggestion is to use that amount of money to get help to get it cleared and organised.

Let's say that your annual fee is $2000. Use that money to hire a professional organiser to help organise and declutter your home and storage unit. Explain to your professional organiser that the aim is to clear the storage unit and therefore save money in the long term. They'll be able to work with you to decide what to keep and what goes. You may even find by selling some of the stuff in the storage unit, you can afford even more time together decluttering and organising.

You might also need to set aside a few hundred dollars to hire a skip. You were going to spend the money anyway, so use the money to get some organisational help. It will be a great investment and you'll have an organised home to boot!

I once had a client booked in, and at the last minute before we'd even met she called to cancel our appointment. She said they couldn't afford my services. Then while on the phone she told me that they'd decided to just hire a storage unit and keep everything in there instead. The issue here wasn't money – they'll spend way more on a storage unit that it would cost them for my services. The issue was being prepared to make the decisions needed to declutter. And that's okay, because there's no use engaging the services of a professional if you're not mentally ready to begin. I'd encourage you to be honest with yourself, so that when you are ready, you take the necessary steps to take back control of your space.

One client had a bathroom that also doubled as a laundry, so it was important to utilise the under-bench storage well. Before I arrived, everything was placed into the cupboards individually. There were bottles of shampoo and conditioner, hair products, nail polish, sanitary products, make up, shaving gear, moisturisers, creams … it was full but not overflowing. They were happy that everything fit inside but found that it got messy almost daily and it was hard to find things at the back.

My favourite bathroom solution for cupboards is open storage baskets that can be lifted out easily. One for hair ties, one for nail polishes, one for shaving stuff, another for sanitary items. You get the idea. This way, when you need something you can pull out the basket and have everything you need at hand. Doing your make up? Pull out that basket, use the products then put it back away easily.

Open containers are one of my 'go-to' products for many uses around the house. So are snap lock bags. Ikea (seeing a theme here?) have an awesome range of quality snap lock bags that I use at almost every job. I've said before they're brilliant for storing accessories for electrical items. I also use them for board games and puzzles.

Every time we finish a new puzzle we grab a snap lock bag and put all the pieces in as we pack up. Sometimes if the box isn't too big I also cut out the picture of the puzzle and put it inside the bag with the pieces, and then get rid of the box. When the kids had lots of smaller puzzles we did this every time and then had a large storage box where the puzzles in snap lock bags lived.

Board games are the same – we use snap lock bags to keep pieces together. Our game of Monopoly, for instance, has several snap locks inside: one for game pieces and dice, one for houses and hotels, one for money and one for properties and game cards. It's easy to pack up and the box is never a mess when we get it out to play. Any game with small pieces is going to be easier with snap lock bags. You can also take games on holidays without risking pieces falling out when you know they're safe inside.

But don't rush out and buy storage before you've decluttered. You'll end up wasting money by buying the wrong solution because you can't accurately see what the overall picture and needs are. Buying storage and organising is probably more fun than decluttering, but if you put the cart before the horse you'll … well, I'm not sure what happens when you put the cart first, but I'm assuming it's a lot more work than having the horse pull it!

Although my advice for clients is customised to their individual space, I do have one particular furniture piece that I find is very versatile and I'd say that 90% of clients end up having in their homes. It's the Ikea piece called a Kallax (formerly Expedit). It's strong, colourful, comes in some great sizes and is simple to assemble. They come in different sizes and can be used in nearly any room of the house. The great thing about this system is you can add drawers, doors and storage tubs into the cubes and you can store just about anything in them.

So aside from my love of cube storage, what else do I recommend?

I suggest to all clients to pick five or six different storage containers and use only those containers around the house. When you buy uniform containers you can stack, interchange and reuse containers wherever you need them at the time. Buy good quality containers and they'll last the long haul; so many of the cheap plastic ones break within a few months. Their wheels fall off, they get cracks or the lids break and then you've wasted your money. I've tried and tested dozens of brands of storage containers and some definitely sit head and shoulders above the pack.

10. Storage

I keep a selection of the best storage containers on the market in my car for when I visit clients. The boot of my car looks like a travelling Ikea store and it is part of the reason I frequent their stores so regularly. When I work with a client, it's so good to get to the organising stage (which is usually the final stage) and be able to set everything up as we want without having to pop out to the shops. Sometimes we need to write a big long shopping list and make a trip, but more often than not I've got everything you need right in the boot of my car. Yep, it's all part of the service!

I recommend having one type of storage for pantry and sticking to that brand. For pantry storage, clear-fronted modular containers are always best because you can see what's inside, so when you write a shopping list it's easy to see what's running low.

I also recommend keeping your fridge storage uniform – again, clear fronted storage works best. Same for your freezer storage (who doesn't love a freezer that stacks and doesn't waste any space!).

'I already have a house full of plastic containers but nothing ever stays in the right one.'

At the risk of sounding like a storage snob, there's nothing very appealing about a playroom of mismatched containers that are different sizes, different colours and missing lids. Visually it's still cluttered because there's no order. There's something relaxing about matching storage containers in a storage unit. Remember, we're not just dealing with the physical clutter, we're also dealing with the visual clutter – which includes things that annoyingly draw your eye, block your view, interrupt your concentration, etc.

My suggestion would be to pick a storage container that is the size and durability you want and buy as many as you need (but no extras). Then either buy a label maker or make labels to put on the boxes. Even clear boxes need labels; it's a visual trigger to stop you putting the wrong things in and it helps children know exactly what goes in each container. I think you'll find that going uniform will really make a difference to how neat storage will appear.

If you have children who aren't as excited about organisation as you are, help them learn by teaching them the benefits. I understand that some people are more naturally organised than others. But in order to live a successful life, organisation is critical, whether in school, the workplace or even in your travels – you'll always be glad you learnt to be organised. I'm not putting forward a case that we all need to be organisational geniuses (that would put me out of work!) but living in chaos never did anyone any favours.

'My storage unit has valuables inside so it's worth keeping.'

Just remember that the value of the items inside is going down by approximately $2000 per year because that's how much you're spending on storing them.

'All this talk of containers makes me think your house looks like a retail store rather than a lived-in home.'

There are such a great variety of storage solutions around that no matter your style, you can find materials and colours that fit in with your décor. Most of the storage in our home is built-in so there are no plastic tubs hanging around the living room.

At our front door we have a mudroom set up, and here we've gone with bold colours against white storage units – instead of hiding them away, they're the focal point of this room. But hidden behind the bright colours is everything we need to grab before we walk out the door or need easy access to – shopping bags, picnic set, bike helmets, wrapping paper, cards, electrical cords, etc.

10. Storage

Having the right storage solutions in your home will make life easier and definitely reduce the day to day stress in your family. But having the wrong storage solutions or trying to organise before you declutter is going to make you think that this organisational stuff just isn't for you. Bottom line, never organise what you can discard.

If you're feeling overwhelmed by the task ahead in your home, having someone in to help is such a valuable investment. You might start decluttering and organising a room but lose steam after half an hour and give up. One of the benefits of having professional help is that they always know what to do next, have years of experience and can give advice on savvy and functional ways to improve the flow of your home.

Simple Tips

- If you currently rent a storage unit, make a decision today to spend the equivalent of the next year's rent on emptying it out and getting some professional organising help.
- Use storage containers for every area of your home. Things are easier to find and easier to put away when they have a home.
- Buy a collection of snap lock bags for puzzles, games, electronics, etc.

Organised Laundry

I've got to admit – I love a well organised laundry. Part of what I love is that it's probably the only room in the whole house with a purely functional purpose. Its value is not in the beauty, space or its lighting – the value is in having it work for you. It's a room we use almost every day and it needs to be robust.

Before you picture my laundry as being a shed-like room, I'd like to say that one day while my hubby was at work, I built storage shelves and hung them on the wall myself. And before I hung them … I painted them bright pink! Imagine his surprise when he arrived home from work! I also have a piece of artwork that my mum made for me when I was a kid hung in the laundry. And I may or may not have also hung some pink paper lanterns from the ceiling … and some butterfly decals on the wall too!

Here are a few quick tips I have for a functional laundry (I'll leave the beautification up to you):

- Have somewhere to hang clothes racks or clothes horses when they're not in use. Hanging them up will keep them out of your way when you're working in the laundry and they'll be easy to access when you need to hang clothes on them.

- If you can fit one of the fold-out or pull-out ironing boards in your laundry – do it! Traditional ironing boards take up a lot of space and tend to be left out if they're used regularly. We have a traditional one and my husband has to get it out every time he needs to use it, which can be a pain. First world problem, but a pain nonetheless.

- Build a shelf to keep washing baskets on or use hooks to hang them from the wall. I've installed a shelf next to my dryer (which is hung above the washing machine) and the three baskets fit in there perfectly; it keeps them out of the way when they're not in use. I hate the visual clutter of washing baskets sitting on the floor of a laundry or living on top of the washing machine.

- Have washing baskets that all match. I don't mean in colour (but feel free if you like). I mean in the shape and style – because being able to nest them inside each other makes life just that bit simpler.

- Teach your children how to put on a load of washing. My boys learnt once they reached primary school and they're pros at it now. I taught them how to decide what to put in together and how to turn things in the right way (does anyone else find their kids take shorts and undies off in one fell swoop and they end up together in the laundry hamper?). They know how to use the machine and how much detergent to use.

Getting Organised

'If it takes less than two minutes, do it now.'

*P*ay now, play later is a core principle in my decision-making and working life. I always pay cash for new cars because I prefer to drive an older car a bit longer while I save up to buy a new one. I'm someone who doesn't often put off chores and I never put off homework as a teenager. I get my teeth into whatever task or job that needs doing – when it's done I'll stop and enjoy a reward.

I think this has also played a part in my ability to keep an organised home. When I see a piece of Lego on the ground, instead of stepping over it I pick it up and put it away. When the junk mail comes I put anything I'm not interested in straight in the recycling bin and put the few that I want to look though in our family 'inbox', ready to read.

Olin Miller says, 'If you want to make an easy job seem mighty hard, just keep putting off doing it.' There are dozens of inspirational quotes that you can find on Instagram and print for the back of the toilet door. But if you don't actually take action, even the quotes will eventually clutter up your brain and you'll be paralysed from starting any decluttering job.

Procrastination is the biggest killer of organisation. If you keep putting off what you can do now, you'll find your pile of things to do will grow exponentially. Alternatively, deciding ahead of time to 'just do it' will put you on the right foot to an ordered home and life.

My friend is a psychologist and she says that a key for some people is to, 'Start seeing yourself as an organised person even if you're not yet there.' Speak like an organised person, do what an organised person would do (i.e. take action on ideas in this book) and before you know it you won't be 'faking' being organised – you'll actually be there!

> *Procrastination is the biggest killer of organisation.*

I cannot advocate enough how important having an organised home is for your mental health. It's game changing. I'm not claiming that getting organised is the beginning and end of mental health treatment, but I am saying that it's an important aspect to pay attention to.

If you are struggling with anxiety, depression or other mental health issues then please speak to your GP. Visit www.beyondblue.org.au and reach out to those around you for help.

Professional organising isn't your first point of contact, but I do know that taking back control of the space you live in can have incredible results on mental health. When you feel like your head is cluttered, cloudy and foggy, it often gets reflected on the space you live in. Living with anxiety or depression is exhausting and even the smallest task can seem insurmountable.

I have the honour of coming into people's homes and helping them create order where chaos has reigned and clear away the cobwebs both physically and mentally. It's not a cure or solution – but it does help.

According to Dr Sherrie Bourg Carter, 'Clutter robs you of mental energy, leaving you feeling anxious, tired and overwhelmed.'

I recently helped a new mum who had a seventeen week old baby who wasn't sleeping, crying for hours and hours per day. She was exhausted and felt the burden that her home had got out of control. When I arrived, she was in her pyjamas and carrying a crying baby. It was lunchtime, but she still hadn't had time for breakfast.

Working with her for a few hours was such a privilege because the difference it made was incredible. Usually I work alongside clients but this time I told her to sit at the bench and I'd do the organising, while she sat with a cuppa and helped curate what was staying and what was going.

I took every single thing out of her kitchen (which her dad had lovingly put away when they moved into the house months earlier, but nothing was in the 'right' spot). Plates were far away from where they serve food; baking dishes were near the sink but not near the oven.

Three hours later I'd literally taken every single item out, decluttered what she didn't use anymore and organised everything so it was easy to access and use. At the end, baby was asleep and mum was thrilled with how her kitchen cupboards and benches looked. The best reward for me was her comment: 'I can't believe how having an organised kitchen has made my brain feel less frazzled. I feel like I can make decisions and my mental clutter is clearing.'

She verbalised the sentiment so many clients have expressed to me over the years. They feel stuck, unengaged with life and overwhelmed. They feel guilty, embarrassed and judged. And something you can guarantee with me is that you'll never be judged or have need for embarrassment. I love the saying, 'Never judge someone because you don't know the journey they have travelled.' This is particularly true when working in people's homes, seeing behind every closed door and inside every cupboard.

I love arriving to clutter and chaos because I can envisage the end result before we start. When clients are embarrassed because their living spaces have got to such a state, I'm itching to get started because I can't wait to see their faces when we finish.

Part of the reason we take before and after photos is because the sense of achievement is worth celebrating. It's so good to be able to share the change with family and friends and to make a commitment to yourself that you'll not let it get back to that state again.

I'm yet to walk into a job and be shocked – I get excited and I love the process as well as the end result of decluttering. If I take a week off, by day five I'm hanging to get into a messy space and tidy it up. I wander around my house trying to find something that can be organised. It's a passion for me and I hope to pass some of that passion onto my clients while I'm with you.

The cleansing that occurs when a good declutter happens in someone's life is incredibly rewarding. Through tears and hugs many people have had breakthrough moments while decluttering their homes. The decluttering seems to help dissolve emotional blockages, allowing honesty and vulnerable to flow. The organising then is like building you up, giving them confidence and peace in who you are.

My aim is to gradually draw the attention away from possessions – to put them in their right order, where they serve your vision and purpose in life. When clutter occurs the attention is disproportionately given to things because they take up so much headspace. Once organised, you should feel your attention is taken away from the 'stuff' you own and your headspace can be given to your loved ones, hobbies, holidays and your health.

Once you've done a full declutter of your home, every space will be feeling fantastic. You'll feel so organised and you'll have an extra spring in your step. So how do we keep our homes in this state? How to we stop the clutter from sneaking back in? Glad you asked! Here are a few of the tips I use.

Everyday Declutter

There is one main principle that helps me keep the house organised, day in and day out. It is a rule my friend told me years and years ago that she'd read in a David Allen book. 'If it takes less than two minutes, do it now.' This above all other motivational or inspirational quotes has made the biggest difference in my organisational life.

It is incredible how many tasks I look at and consider procrastinating, then realise they can be done in less than two minutes. So I do them straight away.

For example:

- Putting away clothes that are on the floor in the bedroom.
- Emptying the dishwasher (time yourself next time – it's so quick).
- Sending a text to a friend.
- Sending a quick email for work.
- Picking up all the cushions on the ground and returning them to the couches.
- Filling a bag with clothes to donate.
- Taking something out of the freezer for dinner the following night.
- Packing away tools after doing a home maintenance job.

Keep this in mind and you'll find the clutter doesn't get out of control because you're always taking small positive steps toward your end goal of peace and organisation.

Weekly Fifteen Minute Declutter

I've mentioned before that fifteen minutes from perfection, is perfect. Well, a good way to test that you're still in that zone is to set the timer for fifteen minutes on a Sunday afternoon and see if you can do it. Fifteen minutes to pack everything back into its home.

Sunday afternoons are a great time to do this because I like to start the week fresh, feeling like there's nothing hanging over my head. I like to know that by the time the kids are in bed on a Sunday night, I'm free to relax and prepare for the week ahead.

One trick I use for the fifteen minute pack up is I grab a washing basket and start in the main room of the house. Anything that is in the family room but doesn't belong there gets thrown in the washing basket. Anything that can be packed up while I'm in there, I do (putting remotes away, for example).

Then I take the washing basket and head into the next room. Here I do the same thing – pick up anything that doesn't belong there and put it in the basket. But while I'm in here, as well as packing up anything in that room I also put away anything from the basket that belongs there.

I continue on through the house: picking up, packing up, putting away. It never takes our family more than fifteen minutes to complete this. And having the timer on makes it a competition (which works well for my super-competitive family!).

Seasonal Declutter

At the start of each season (summer, autumn, winter and spring), spend a day decluttering as a family. If you have children this can include going through their wardrobes to take out anything they've grown out of and passing them on. Toys or games they've grown out of can go. It's like a refresher day to get you back to a fresh clean slate.

Along with this I strongly encourage clients to use their local council rubbish collection. This is paid for as part of your rates so you've already paid for it – might as well use it! Now, don't wait until you have stuff to get rid of before you book it. Just book one each for the start of March and September (or whenever works for you) and then you can figure out what you'll put out there. Even if you only end up putting a few things out, better they are picked up and out of your home than you collecting a massive pile and needing to pay for a tip run.

Now, note that this recommendation isn't for those decluttering for the first time – it's for once you're living an organised life. When you're starting out and doing a big declutter, the council 1m cube allowance you get isn't nearly enough. When you start I'd suggest at least a 3m cube skip (and I've had clients fill three of those in less than twenty-four hours, so be prepared!)

'Sounds like I'll be spending every weekend decluttering!'

At first, you might spend a few weekends as part of the process, but it's worth it because once it's done you can slip into maintenance mode. It takes much less time to keep organised than to get organised in the first place. Good systems in place, like mentioned above, will keep you on the right path.

It's kind of like maintaining a garden – you can do a little bit each weekend and keep on top of it, but if you completely neglect your whole garden it will take you a few weekends of hard work to get it back to acceptable. What I do with people is like the *Backyard Blitz* of homes. We work hard initially for however many sessions are needed, and then we scale right back and I put the right tools in your hands to manage it.

When I was talking about how mental health and clutter have a close relationship, you may have been thinking that it was hard enough to pick up this book and read it – there's no way your mental health is stable enough or strong enough to actually do everything you're reading about. And that might be your reality right now. I'd suggest you talk to your psychologist or counsellor or GP and let them know you're thinking about starting the decluttering and organising process. Ask what they think. Ask for advice about how you could go about it.

You may find that hiring a professional organiser for one session a week across a few months is the right way to go about it, rather than trying to get it completely done in two weeks or attempting it on your own.

There's never shame in asking for help – that's what those of us in the service industry are there for. We want to help people move forward and experience success.

I personally have a cleaner come to our home once a fortnight for two hours. She's amazing and she helps our family run smoothly. I'm not someone who enjoys cleaning at all – but she does, so I pay her to help us in that area.

I do the same for others when it comes to organisational areas of the home. It's like calling a plumber when a tap isn't working. You could probably work out how to do it via YouTube, but it's safer and more sensible to call in a professional.

'Sounds like decluttering can become an expensive process with hiring skips and working with a professional organiser.'
If you asked my clients, every single one would say it has been a great investment and they never would have achieved such great results by themselves.

It does require an investment from you in time, energy and headspace, as well as financially – but the cost of not taking this step is so much higher than taking it. And stepping in half-heartedly will result in a yo-yo diet of decluttering and then accumulating clutter again.

Sometimes in life you need to just draw a line in the sand and decide you're going to make a change. This is one of those times.

Simple Tips

- Book a council hard rubbish collection today.
- Grab a washing basket and walk around the house for fifteen minutes, putting things back in their homes.
- If it takes less than two minutes, do it now.

Minimalism

'I wish I did this years ago.'

There is a freedom that comes from having less that isn't believed until it's experienced. There is momentum growing around the minimalism movement and it's exciting to be a part of it.

It used to be that if you wanted to live the simple lifestyle, you'd buy a plot of land to live remotely and enjoy a slower pace of life. A simpler life certainly is very appealing, but moving out of the city isn't for everyone.

Is it possible to work a corporate job, have a modern day family and yet still embrace minimalism? There certainly are a lot of advantages to tempt you …

But first, what is minimalism?

I love the definition given by Joshua Field Millburn and Ryan Nicodemus – I met them last year and they speak with clarity around the story of minimalism.

> Minimalism is a tool that can assist you in finding freedom. Freedom from fear. Freedom from worry. Freedom from overwhelm. Freedom from guilt. Freedom from depression. Freedom from the trappings of the consumer culture that we've built our lives around. Real freedom.[4]

> Minimalism is a lifestyle that helps people question what things add value to their lives. By clearing the clutter from life's path, we can all make room for the most important aspects of life: health, relationships, passion, growth and contribution.[5]

The media send us mixed messages around minimalism. You'll see an advert where a couple relax on the beach with no one around them – they look so peaceful. But the ad will be for something that a company wants you to buy. They tempt us with one lifestyle then try to sell us something completely different.

We're sold the story that road trips, weekends away and beach getaways are all within our reach, then we're bombarded with advertising for *more* and *better*. More stuff, better stuff, upgrades – all of which lead in the opposite direction to a simple life.

Living with less is like giving yourself permission to be grateful for what you have. I find that when I have less clutter around me, I have an increased sense of gratitude. Mindfulness and gratitude are two of the greatest gifts we can give ourselves and our families. Minimalism at its core is a move towards these two values.

---

4. 'What is Minimalism?', The Minimalists, <http://www.theminimalists.com/minimalism/>
5. 'Minimalism: An Elevator Pitch', The Minimalists, <http://www.theminimalists.com/pitch/>

12. Minimalism

My dad gave me advice when I was entering adulthood – he said to hold my possessions and wealth in an open hand. I've reflected often on what that looks like and what the implications are for me in choosing to embrace that value.

It means that I understand my wealth and possessions aren't a reflection of the quality of person that I am. It means regardless of how much wealth passes through my hands, my value is not determined by money or possessions. This means that generosity is never a difficult thing to do and I can never be stolen from.

My husband and I both want to live with a spirit of generosity, and the most powerful generosity occurs in the secret places. When we give without anyone knowing, that's when our true motives are tested. When we ourselves have need, but still choose generosity, our reliance on and security in money is tested.

I think the best thing about holding our possessions with an open hand is that my possessions don't own me. They don't make me happy when I'm feeling sad. They don't make me feel worthwhile when I doubt my value. They don't give me comfort when I'm lonely. They don't give me confidence when I'm insecure. Those things, for me, come from a much deeper place; they are grounded in my faith and relationship with God. Don't let stuff fill the spaces in your life they were never designed to fit.

I read a great quote this week: 'The best things in life aren't things at all.' Having freedom from your 'stuff' is priceless.

When you go away on holidays or go camping, do you ever think to yourself how happy you are and then realise you don't have 90% of your stuff with you? Do you sometimes wonder how long in a week you spend looking after 'stuff'? Sometimes I wonder if less stuff equals more life …

Minimalism doesn't mean that you give away everything you own, move into a caravan, start a blog and live with twenty-six items of clothing. These things might be part of the journey for you, but there's no blueprint for how minimalism looks for each person.

You may start by asking yourself the question, 'Do I love this?' when you declutter your home. Peter Walsh says, 'The stuff you own should help you create the life you want.' And if it doesn't, you probably don't need it in your home. Decluttering is almost always the first step to minimalism.

I have clients tell me constantly that they don't have enough built-in storage in their homes. I have felt that about my home at times too, but the issue isn't that we don't have enough storage; it's that we have too much stuff. It's so much easier to just build storage, fill the garage or rent a storage unit than commit ourselves to decluttering our lives. But when we do, it's like a weight lifts from our burdened shoulders.

> *Mindfulness and gratitude are two of the greatest gifts we can give ourselves and our families.*

I recently worked with a beautiful client who, five years prior, had been through a difficult separation. She'd both emotionally and physically shut the door to that stage of her life. There was a room off her garage that contained everything from that period. Anything that reminded her of the pain was put behind a closed door. By the time I got called in she hadn't been inside the room for years. She had forgotten what was in there.

12. Minimalism

We spent two days taking out every single item and we filled up two huge skip bins. The lady I said goodbye to after two days was a different woman to the one I met on the first morning. She seemed to have regained her self-assurance and self-confidence. I received a touching email from her daughter the following day and I want to share it with you:

> Amy, even from when I first contacted you through email I sensed you would have the gentle but direct approach needed for my mum. You've worked your magic and taken a huge burden off her shoulders. She spoke so highly of you when telling me about the experience and I could hear in her voice how much lighter she felt after achieving this clear out. She's now excited and more confident to take the next step for the future, thank you for your part in this.

Whether you choose to declutter yourself or work with a professional organiser – or if you completely ignore the issue until one day you pass away – someone at some point is going to declutter your stuff.

Nobody is going to get up at your funeral and talk about how nice the silver was in your crystal cabinet. No one is going to talk about how your handbag collection was always on trend or how great it was you always carried the most current device. They're going to get up and talk about the time they spent with you. They'll share silly stories of family get-togethers and road trips taken. They'll speak of your character and values and the legacy you'll leave.

I don't want to linger here longer than necessary but sometimes it's good to be reminded that silver and gold won't accompany us to the grave.

> 'Minimalism is not subtraction for the sake of subtraction.
> Minimalism is subtraction for the sake of focus.' – Anonymous

If you think of minimalism as a movement that takes things away from you, then most people would run away. Nobody likes being taken from; it's disempowering. But what if you saw it as a movement of adding focus? Focus on the important things and people and places in life. That's way more appealing – because that's what it does. It gives focus, freedom and peace through embracing the important things in life.

Clutter robs people of so many things. It robs you of time, space, peace, creativity and it gives absolutely nothing back. So it's time to reclaim your home and life.

'Minimalist homes feel clinical and cold.'

Minimalism doesn't mean giving away anything of beauty and living in a small white unfurnished home; but a minimalist home won't feel cluttered.

One distinctive characteristic of a minimal home is a sense of peace and order you feel when you walk into the space. There's room to breathe and think and relax. You still embrace colour, beauty and decoration; you're just intentional about it. We have some big pieces of art on our walls that I absolutely adore. I had blank walls for about a year before I found what I was looking for and now they bring such character to our space and I love it. They don't take away from my living room because they're big – they add to it because they're intentional.

I can't tell you how many people have commented that my home feels peaceful. I've often reflected on what causes them to say that. It's not because it's quiet – my two boys are very boisterous. It's not because it's perfectly styled – I'm not an interior designer. It's not because it's a modern space; the house itself is about seventy years old.

My conclusion is that by embracing minimalism and organisation they don't feel 'shouted at' by my possessions. They feel the sense of space we create. They are able to stop and feel at peace.

Like all movements, there will be people who decide to live what we'd consider a radical expression. If that's you, then go for it. There isn't room for judgement of things like this in life. But also understand that choosing to have a spare room that simply has a bed in it is choosing minimal. Buying a home that's the size you need rather than as big as you can afford is minimal. Having a curated wardrobe and wearing what you own is also minimal. Being a vegan can be an expression of minimalism, as can having a sugar free diet. Start where you're comfortable and step by step, aim to release the tight grip consumerism has on us.

'I work hard and I deserve to buy things that make me feel comfortable.'

I would probably just reframe this to say you do work hard and you have the choice to buy things that make you feel comfortable. Again, mindfulness is at play here. Feeling like we deserve things in life because we work hard can go against living with wealth and possessions in an open hand. But feeling like we're constantly deprived isn't ideal either!

I believe there is a balance in all of this that is expressed differently for each person and family. Again, we're trying to move away from being possessed by our possessions to the freedom that having our value and worth intrinsically derived will bring.

When I work with clients, we don't focus solely on minimalism – we focus on decluttering and organising to a level that fits with the life they want to live. If you're interested in exploring minimalism further I'd suggest you subscribe to my podcast *The Art of Decluttering* for continued growth and inspiration in this area.

I can't encourage you enough to practice gratefulness in your life. When you're grateful for what you have, your satisfaction with life is increased and your general happiness explodes.

Joshua Becker of Becoming Minimalist says, 'Materialism is, after all, the natural behaviour born out of discontent with the possessions that we own.'

And if you're not yet ready to embark on minimalism, next time you're on holidays take note of how you feel when you're surrounded by less. Do you feel less pressure? Do you feel more spontaneous? How does your usually busy and cluttered mind feel?

I love the principles surrounding minimalism, which is why I've dedicated a whole chapter to it here. It's not something you can teach someone in a book, but it's a lifestyle you pursue.

Decluttering and organisation are the first steps to taking back control of your home and bringing back the peace and order that you so desperately desire. Take these two steps first and see where the journey leads.

Afterword

Where to from here?

Congratulations! You've just finished the first step in getting your home decluttered and organised. Hopefully your head and heart now align with the *why* of organising your home and you feel like you've gained some helpful tools.

I'm so proud of you – because your intentions are good. You want the best for your life and for your family. You have the desire to go against the grain of consumerism and to simplify your life so you can best enjoy your friends and world around you. Whether you plan on embracing a minimalist lifestyle or whether you'd just like to park your car in the garage, you're on the right track.

I don't want this to be just another book you read, recommend to friends and never do anything about. You've invested in this book. You've invested time, headspace and money – and the great thing is, I believe it was a solid investment.

If you begin to follow some of my advice, tips and tricks I know that your return on investment will be great. Pick one area that you think you're ready to declutter and then organise. Or work your way through the book, chapter by chapter. I've intentionally designed the book so that once you've read it cover to cover, you can easily go back and follow the guide of a chapter in isolation.

Talk to your friends about organising, and encourage each other on the journey. It's so nice to have people to travel with in life. If you see a neighbour or friend who is drowning in clutter, don't judge them – buy them a copy of this book and offer to help them out.

We're all better people when we live in a community, and part of what I love about my career is I get to be that someone for so many women. I get to be an honest friend and I get to be their personal cheerleader as they make progress. Sometimes I'm a shoulder to cry on and sometimes I'm the only person they'll let see inside their bathroom cupboard or wardrobe. Women are amazing at juggling so many things in life – and that juggle is made so much easier by living an organised life.

So thank you. Thank you for seeing this book as valuable enough to give your time to read it. The reason I wrote it is because I saw each and every reader as valuable enough to spend time putting my thoughts down on paper.

Remember, you're not defined by your possessions! Living a clutter-free and organised life is within reach and you can totally do it!

Enjoy the journey and congratulations,

About the Author

Amy Revell is born and bred in Melbourne, Australia.

Growing up as the eldest of five girls, Amy became a natural leader in all spheres of life. Engaging in volunteer work from the age of seven and starting her first business at the age of eight, Amy has a strong social conscience and desire to help people be the best they can be.

Amy has always been a super organised person, and this natural gift has developed into a successful, engaging and fun business, helping women better organise their homes and lives. From having the most organised bedroom as a child to being the first point of call when friends need home advice, she enjoys walking into cluttered homes and finding order and peace amidst the chaos.

Clients often remark that her non-judgemental and sensitive approach means that instead of being embarrassed of their homes, they feel supported and inspired to make positive changes. One client said, 'It's like having your sister around to help you get organised.' Professional organising is a passion for Amy and she's constantly reminded of the environmental, psychological and financial benefits to living an organised life.

Amy is a wife and mum of two active boys who even keep their rooms clean without being asked! They enjoy socialising with friends, playing board games, going on holidays and being involved in their local church.

the art of decluttering

WORKING WITH AMY

Podcast

*I*ndustry leaders and professional organisers Amy Revell and Kirsty Famgia bring you *The Art of Decluttering* podcast.

We have a passion to transform the world through intentional living by equipping people to clear the clutter in their heads, hearts and homes.

Our style is conversational, informative and we love having a good laugh together.

Search *The Art of Decluttering* on your podcast app, subscribe and never miss an episode.

The Art of Decluttering Services

So where do you start in creating a home of peace and calm?

From single sessions to entire home packages, there's something to suit everyone.

The Art of Decluttering team have experience and knowledge that are incredibly valuable. Amy and her business partner, Kirsty, along with their team love walking into chaos and helping establish peace, calm and routines for every family. So get in contact and be ready to transform you home from chaos to calm.

amy@theartofdecluttering.com.au

www.theartofdecluttering.com.au

Amy as a Speaker

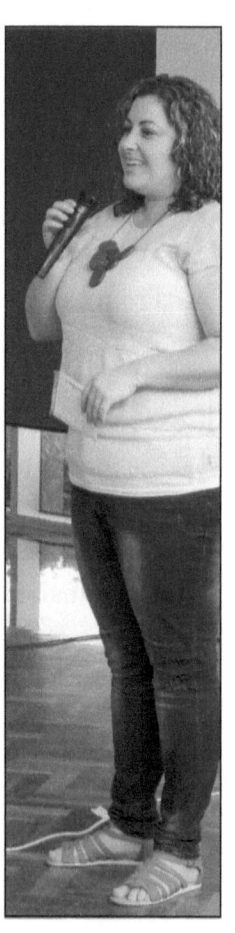

'Amy must have that part of the brain that I was missing. Seriously, she graced through my home with warmth, understanding and didn't just do what she thought was best. She asks smart questions on how our spaces are used.

'Amy came into my disorganised life and transformed the clutter to a home that's liveable, versatile and organised. I'm a mum of four and everything Amy put in place has worked and adapted to the needs of the kids.'
– Paige Sonsie, satisfied client

For more information or to make a booking, contact Amy Revell:

0438 659 658

www.theartofdecluttering.com.au

amy@theartofdecluttering.com.au

*A*my is a leading professional organiser in Australia. As a successful author, podcaster and blogger Amy loves equipping women go find freedom through decluttering and organising their homes.

Amy is a great choice as keynote speaker for your event, whether community or church event, in-store workshop or business conference.

As well as physically decluttering with clients, the mindset and habit changes that Amy teaches are life transformational and will change the way your home runs forever.

Appearing regularly on TV, radio and in print, Amy is an industry leader with a passion to share her message of life transformation.

Keynote Topic

*4 Biggest Secrets to Overcoming Clutter
in Your Home without the Stress*

- Why clutter builds up in the first place.
- How to declutter your way to freedom.
- Tools for decluttering and organising.

> 'Amy is exceptional at what she does … she can transform chaos into organisation with a smooth easy system. Nothing is too difficult for Amy and this is all done with a big smile and lots of laughs.'
> – Emily Lavis, satisfied client

"Take joy in what you have by decluttering what you don't need"

"Minimalism gives focus, freedom and peace through embracing the important things in life"

"In order to live a life of **success**, organisation is crucial. Whether in school, the workplace or even in your travels – you'll always be glad you learnt to be organised."

BEFORE

AFTER

"Gradually draw attention away from possessions – put them in their right order, where they serve your vision and purpose in life"

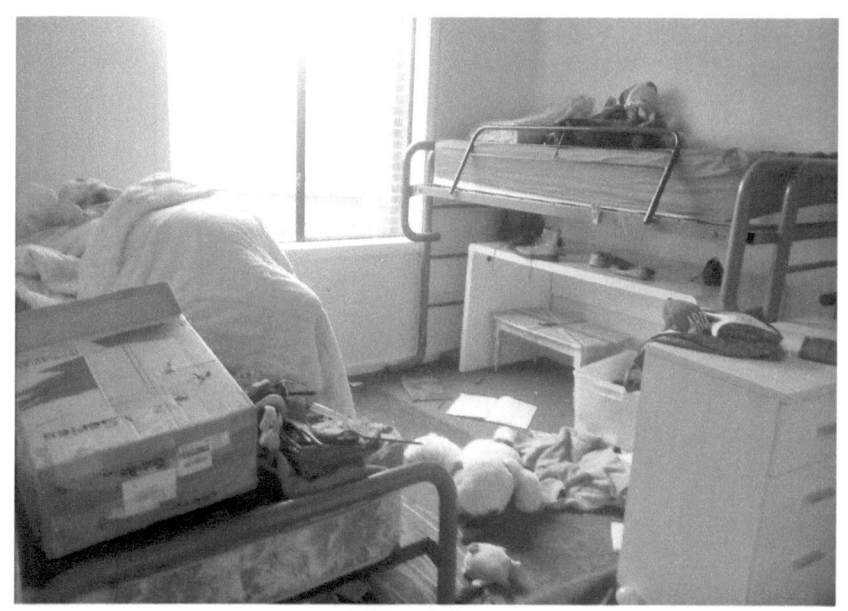

BEFORE

AFTER

"It's possible to create **order** where chaos has reigned"

BEFORE

AFTER

"Peace and calm are a treasured gift in our fast paced world"

BEFORE

AFTER

"Decluttering and organisation are the first steps to taking back **control** of your home"

BEFORE

AFTER

"How glorious it is to rest in a home that you've taken the time to organise"

BEFORE

AFTER

"A decluttered home means that there's room to breathe, to think and to relax"

"It's time to reinstate peace and order in your home"

www.ingramcontent.com/pod-product-compliance
Lightning Source LLC
Chambersburg PA
CBHW021106080526
44587CB00010B/406